The ID CaseBook

Case Studies in Instructional Design

Peggy A. Ertmer
Purdue University

James Quinn
Oakland University

With a Foreword by
David Jonassen
Pennsylvania State University

Merrill,
an imprint of Prentice Hall
Upper Saddle River, New Jersey   *Columbus, Ohio*

To my five most favorite people, Dave, Mark, Emilie, Laura, Scott—Peggy Ertmer
To my parents, Charles and Carmel Quinn—James Quinn

Library of Congress Cataloging-in-Publication Data

Ertmer, Peggy A.
    The ID casebook : case studies in instructional design / Peggy A.
  Ertmer, James Quinn.
        p. cm.
    Includes bibliographical references
    ISBN 0-13-859042-7
    1. Instructional systems—Design—Case studies.   I. Quinn, James.
        II. Title.
LB1028.38.E78   1999
371.3—dc21   98-27268
                                                                               CIP

Editor: Debra A. Stollenwerk
Production Editor: Mary Harlan
Design Coordinator: Diane C. Lorenzo
Text Design and Production Supervision: Custom Editorial Productions, Inc.
Cover Designer: Tanya Burgess
Cover Photo: © Westlight
Production Manager: Pamela D. Bennett
Director of Marketing: Kevin Flanagan
Marketing Manager: Suzanne Stanton
Marketing Coordinator: Krista Groshong

This book was set in Avant Garde by Custom Editorial Productions, Inc., and was printed and
bound by R.R. Donnelley & Sons Company. The cover was printed by Phoenix Color Corp.

© 1999 by Prentice-Hall, Inc.
Upper Saddle River, New Jersey 07458

Printed in the United States of America

10 9 8   7 6 5 4 3

ISBN: 0-13-859042-7

Prentice-Hall International (UK) Limited, *London*
Prentice-Hall of Australia Pty. Limited, *Sydney*
Prentice-Hall of Canada, Inc., *Toronto*
Prentice-Hall Hispanoamericana, S. A., *Mexico*
Prentice-Hall of India Private Limited, *New Delhi*
Prentice-Hall of Japan, Inc., *Tokyo*
Simon & Schuster Asia Pte. Ltd., *Singapore*
Editora Prentice-Hall do Brasil, Ltda., *Rio de Janeiro*

Foreword

This book is long overdue. I think everyone would agree with that. Whether your underlying epistemology and pedagogy are objectivist or constructivist, situated or abstract, tried-and-true or new-and-different, you have probably been looking for a collection of instructional design cases for years. For all of you, *The ID CaseBook* should fulfill a need in your instructional design courses, regardless of your preferred methodology.

The *CaseBook* is flexible. It can be used in introductory courses (my preference) or in capstone design courses after students have learned about design principles and theories. Or it may be used across a number of courses to situate principles and theories learned throughout a design program.

The *CaseBook* is flexible because it can support different forms of learning and instruction for instructional design. The cases in this book can be used as examples in traditional design courses or as contexts for constructivist courses. In either situation, the cases will enhance students' understanding of how instructional design gets done. These cases are authentic. They are real-world examples of instructional design practice.

The *CaseBook* is flexible because the cases are diverse. They represent a variety of contexts, content, and instructional design processes as well as a variety of writing styles. They represent the inherent complexity of the instructional design process as well as its generalizability across contexts. Some cases are more complex than others. But so are design problems. Overall, I think the *CaseBook* presents an effective balance of complexity and difficulty.

The ID CaseBook models what it advocates. The student version of the *CaseBook* presents the problems. The Instructor's Guide (available to instructors) supports the teaching of the course. It provides guidelines and suggestions (scaffolding and coaching) for instructors who are new to teaching with cases.

The authentic nature of cases as learning experiences presents a series of challenges to instructional designers and academics. For example, the cases represent ill-structured design problems that have multiple goals and solutions. That may be troublesome for some, because it means that their solution may not be the best. But the primary challenge of most forms of student-centered pedagogy is to relinquish authority, primarily intellectual authority over the content. I believe that is a benefit because it compels students and faculty to acknowledge and consider multiple perspectives on the design process. From solving design problems, students will quickly learn that instructional design is not as prescriptive a science as some of our theories suggest. Any given model or method may represent an effective solution to only a limited number of design problems. No model represents an appropriate solution in all situations. Because the problems have multiple solutions and solution paths, instructors and students must at least consider alternative perspectives and solutions. That's reality.

And now for the really big challenge—assessment. You cannot perform item analysis on these cases. Reliability coefficients cannot be calculated. Even if they could, they would not be significant (statistically or conceptually). Perhaps the greatest challenge to teachers is how to assess learning from cases. In the real world, you are required to evaluate instruction and instructional designers. What makes a good instructional design? When assessing instructional design students, you must first be clear about this in your own mind. Ultimately, we are concerned with whether our students are able to transfer the skills that they have learned to new instructional design problems. No designer in the real world gets paid for answering multiple-choice questions. We want to know if they can design. So, we need to present design problems and assess learners' performance. That requires us to articulate criteria or rubrics for what makes a good solution. And it also requires learners to justify, defend, and argue for the actions they suggest. Did they consider contextual factors? Did they always use the same design model? Could they articulate appropriate assessment methods?

There are rich but complex assessment opportunities in the solutions to the cases represented in *The ID CaseBook*. One possibility is to have students write their own cases and plausible solutions as evidence of their understanding of the instructional design process. Real generative learning is more than relating someone else's interpretations to your own. Creating and designing new examples of any learning outcome is what makes learning truly generative.

Selecting and using these cases (and others which you or your students might develop) will engage your students in acting like instructional designers. I believe that *The ID CaseBook* provides an invaluable resource for supporting your efforts and for promoting and diffusing significant change in the instructional design field. That's enough for me.

David Jonassen

Preface

It is possible that a person who is good at learning something from the book will not know how to deal with a realistic situation. Like some of the designers in the cases we discussed, we may have a master's or doctoral degree in instructional design, yet still not deal with a situation well. We need the opportunity to practice what we learn in our books.

So began a graduate student at the end of one of our instructional design (ID) courses, when asked to describe the value of analyzing and discussing ID case studies. This student's comments summarize our primary purpose for this text: to provide students with opportunities to practice what they learn in class; to bridge the gap between the complex reality of the design world and the isolated principles taught in traditional textbooks.

Although ID educators have recognized the potential of the case method of teaching in the education of instructional designers for a number of years, there have been relatively few materials available that help ID educators actually implement this approach in their courses. Most educators do not have the time or expertise to create ID cases for their courses yet would use such cases if they were available. This *ID CaseBook* offers ID educators a rich resource of authentic design problems that can be used in either introductory or advanced design courses, as well as in more specialized courses related to any of the specific design steps or issues. Because of our commitment to the case method of instruction, we felt a sense of urgency to make case materials readily available so that ID educators could begin to use cases in their classes, immediately as well as relatively easily.

▶ Conceptual Framework

Our book arises out of a view of ID as a complex, ill-structured domain of knowledge, for which there is a methodology and a set of guidelines but not a single set of procedures that will guarantee success. This view of ID recognizes that professional ID competence requires more than technical expertise. Although some design situations may involve well-structured and clearly defined problems that will benefit from the application of a set of technical procedures, many more situations are ill-structured and poorly defined. In addition to the necessary technical skills and knowledge, such situations depend on the artistry and skill of ID professionals to operate creatively and effectively in these ambiguous, uncertain, and open-ended contexts. Given the constraints of time and other resources, how does an instructor convey the complexity and ill-structured nature of ID while at the same time teach the technical skills that are prerequisite for ID practice? We believe, as do many others, that the case teaching approach has the potential to help bridge this gap by situating the learning of technical ID skills within authentic contexts.

There are probably as many definitions of case-based instruction as there are ways of implementing it. In this text, we use an approach to case studies that is based on the business school model—that is, case studies are problem-centered descriptions of design situations, developed from the actual experiences of instructional designers.

The cases in this book are designed to be dilemma oriented—that is, each case ends before the solution is clear. Students are expected to evaluate the available evidence, to judge alternative interpretations and actions, and to experience the uncertainty that often accompanies design decisions. In particular, we hope that by analyzing the cases presented in this book, ID students will learn how to identify ID problems and subproblems, recognize the importance of context in resolving such problems, and develop, justify, and test alternative plans for resolving ID problems.

Organization

The ID CaseBook is divided into three parts. In the introduction (Part I), we provide students with suggestions and strategies for how to approach *learning* from case-based instruction. Although it is our experience that students are typically excited about using case studies in instruction, because of their unfamiliarity with this approach, they often feel a little apprehensive as well. We have found that by providing helpful suggestions up front, students' initial concerns are considerably lessened.

Part II includes 24 cases situated in a variety of educational and business contexts. Case titles typically bear the name of the instructional designer in the case. Cases are arranged alphabetically, by title, to avoid alerting students as to the nature of the issues addressed. This decision was based on our belief that students need to be able to identify and define presenting problems before they can begin to solve them. To ease the selection process for instructors, however, a matrix is provided in the *Instructor's Guide* that allows instructors to see the particular issues and subissues of each case, as well as the specific content and context of each.

In Part III, we invite students to reflect on their own case learning experiences, and also, as beginning instructional designers, on the usefulness of the case method as a teaching and learning strategy. In addition, we invite students to explore some future possibilities for case-based instruction, in particular—the use of the World Wide Web as a delivery medium.

❱ **Features**

The *ID CaseBook* consists of 24 ID case studies, with individual cases being contributed by members of the ID community. Each case is based on a real experience that these authors, their colleagues, or their students have encountered. By compiling these experiences into one book, we can offer students the combined professional experiences of some of the best scholars and practitioners in our field.

Each case consists of a case narrative and a set of questions designed to invoke ID practice. The *case narrative* includes relevant background information for the case, including the problem context, key players, available resources, and existing constraints. In addition, each case includes *relevant data* presented in a variety of forms and formats. The set of questions at the end of each case—*Invoking ID Practice*—provide focus for students' analysis process. These questions may require students to identify and discuss issues, consider the issues from multiple perspectives, develop a plan of action to resolve problems, and/or specify possible consequences resulting from their recommended plan.

The *Instructor's Guide* that accompanies this book includes:

Case Matrix: a summary matrix that allows instructors to see, at a glance, the particular issues and subissues of each case

Teaching Suggestions: ideas for instructors regarding the different ways the cases can be used with different levels of students

Case Overview: a brief description of the case, including the "big idea" students should glean from the case

Case Objectives: the specific focus of the case (the supporting concepts/principles learners should use in analyzing the case issues); the knowledge, skills, and/or attitudes students should gain from their case analyses and discussions

Preliminary Analysis Questions: supplementary questions that the instructor can choose to use in assisting students to focus on issues in the case

Debriefing Guidelines: suggestions from the case authors regarding how to think about the case.

It is our hope that the combined features of the *ID CaseBook* and the *Instructor's Guide* will provide both students and instructors with a challenging and rewarding learning experience. We continue to view this whole venture as a work-in-progress. If you or your students have suggestions for future editions, we'd love to hear from you! Our e-mail addresses are:

pertmer@purdue.edu
quinn@oakland.edu

▶ Acknowledgments

Throughout this endeavor we have benefited from support, advice, and encouragement from a number of individuals, including the contributing authors, enthusiastic colleagues, understanding family members, thoughtful students, careful secretaries, an outstanding editor, and exceptional reviewers. Without the contributions of all these people, this book would not have been possible.

First, we would like to thank all the authors who contributed to this volume. Quite simply, without them there would be no book! They made our work interesting, enjoyable and relatively painless. One of the benefits to us, in creating a contributed text, was having the opportunity to interact with these colleagues—some of whom we've never met, others whom we rarely see, but also those who work down the hall. We firmly believe that each author has added something unique to the text and sincerely appreciate the time each gave to develop and revise their cases.

Our current and past students have been influential in shaping many of the details of the text, particularly in making suggestions for how to think about the case-learning process. We are also grateful to our colleagues who were willing to pilot the cases in their courses and to provide valuable formative feedback that improved numerous aspects of the cases.

We especially would like to thank our editor, Debbie Stollenwerk, and the rest of the production crew at Merrill/Prentice Hall. Debbie played a key role throughout the development process—initially by encouraging our efforts and helping us clarify our goals, and later by guiding the refinement of our ideas. We were also assisted in the design and development process by the insights and suggestions from a number of reviewers, including John C. Belland, The Ohio State University; Wallace Hannum, University of North Carolina–Chapel Hill; Sarah Huyvaert, Eastern Michigan University; David Jonassen, Pennsylvania State University; Mable Kinzie, University of Virginia; Gary R. Morrison, Wayne State University; Tim Newby, Purdue University; John Ronghua Ouyang, Kennesaw State University; Brenda S. Peters, The College of Saint Rose; Tillman J. Ragan, The University of Oklahoma; Gregory C. Sales, Seward Learning Systems, Inc; and Robert Tennyson, University of Minnesota.

Contents

Part I

Introduction

by Peggy A. Ertmer
and
James Quinn

Although case methods have been used in business, law, and medicine for over 100 years, it is likely that this will be one of your first experiences with the case approach. This may give rise to a wide range of feelings—excitement, nervousness, curiosity, intimidation. In addition, you'll probably have a lot of questions: How do I analyze a case? How will I know if I've done it right? Where will I find the information and resources I need to solve the case problems? Although it is our experience that students are typically excited about using case studies in instruction, because of their unfamiliarity with this approach, they often feel a little apprehension as well. We've written this section, addressed to you specifically, because we have found that initial concerns can be lessened by describing, up front, the types of tasks you will be expected to complete, as well as some of the adjustments you may need to make in your current "learning mindsets." As one of our former students noted:

> In my opinion, if students were told up front that this style of learning (case-based instruction) feels slow and cumbersome at first, and that they should read and re-read the information in the case a couple of times, do what they need to visualize and better understand the scenarios—it might be easier to adjust to. I think case-based learning is a valuable and interactive method that just takes a different mindset than most students are used to.

We think this student makes two excellent suggestions: tell students what this approach "feels" like and tell them how to actually "do" it (i.e., analyze a case). Although we don't really believe that we *can* tell you exactly how it feels to learn from cases or how you must go about analyzing a case, we offer a few thoughts and suggestions related to these two elements of the case-learning experience. We begin with suggested strategies and procedures for analyzing a case and then provide suggestions on how to adopt a "facilitative" mindset so that you get the most from your case-learning experience.

Strategies for Analyzing a Case

There are probably a variety of ways a case study could be effectively analyzed. We offer the following as one possibility:

1

1. **Understand the context in which the case is being analyzed and discussed**. If your instructor is using this text to supplement another, then the cases will probably be used to provide "real-world" examples of the content or design steps you've discussed. This context can help focus your attention on relevant issues, questions, and concerns related to your readings and other coursework. Also, each case includes a set of focusing questions at the end. You may want to read these questions first, as a way to "prime the mental pump." Reading case questions before you read the case may help you read more meaningfully and more effectively.

2. **Read the case**. Your first reading should probably be fairly quick, just to get a general sense of what the case is about—the key players, main issues, context, and so on.

3. **Read the case again**. Your second (and subsequent) reading(s) should be much slower: taking notes, considering multiple perspectives, thinking about alternative solutions and consequences. The benefits you reap from your case analysis will relate to how much time you spend—not necessarily reading, but reflecting on what you have read.

4. **Analyze the case**. This is probably the "fuzziest" and thus most overwhelming step of the whole case-analysis process. Assuming that you have already identified the facts of the case, relevant information, key players, context, and resources and constraints, we recommend that you complete the following steps during your analysis:
   ‣ Identify the key issues in the cases.
   ‣ Consider main issues from the perspectives of the key players.
   ‣ Generate a list of potential solutions related to each issue.
   ‣ Specify possible consequences of each solution.
   ‣ Weigh the advantages and limitations to each solution and make a recommendation for action.

5. **Actively participate in class discussion**. The case class is a learning community—together you, your instructor, and your peers are working to gain a more complete understanding of the case situation and possible solutions. It is important that you be an active participant as well as an active listener. You must listen carefully to what others are saying so that your questions and contributions can move the discussion along. Coming prepared to class is critical to your ability to participate in, and benefit from, the case-learning experience.

6. **Reflect on the case-learning experience**. Boud, Keogh, and Walker (1985) stated that in any learning experience, reflection is needed at various points: at the *start*, in a preparatory phase when you start to explore what is required of you, as you become aware of the demands of the situation and the resources you bring to bear;

during the experience, as a way of dealing with the vast array of inputs and coping with the feelings generated; and *after* the experience, as you attempt to make sense of it. The case method provides fertile ground for facilitating a reflective approach to learning. Starting with the first step in the analysis process, as you consider the context in which you are studying a case, you engage in a reflective process. As you implement your analysis approach, you complete four activities that Noordhoff and Kleinfeld (1990) state are inherent in a "reflective approach" to design:

▶ Naming and framing situations and issues
▶ Identifying goals and appraising their worth
▶ Sorting images, selecting strategies, and spinning out consequences
▶ Reflecting on effects and redesigning one's practice

Finally, at the end of a case analysis, reflection helps you make sense of your experiences with the case and deepen your understanding. By reflecting on both the products and the processes of your learning experiences, you gain insights essential to improving future performances. Reflection can link past and future actions by providing you with information about the strategies you used (learning process) and the outcomes you achieved (learning products). It allows you to take stock of what has happened and to prepare yourself for future action.

▶ Developing a Facilitative Mindset

In all forms of professional education, a fundamental goal exists: to help a novice "think like" a member of the profession (Shulman, 1992). Kitchener and King (1990) indicated that reflective thinking matures with both age and experience. They listed the following qualities as characteristic of mature reflective thinkers: viewing situations from multiple perspectives, searching for alternative explanations of events, and using evidence to support or evaluate a decision or position. These qualities form an essential part of the mindset that we believe facilitates learning from case studies. We provide additional guidelines below, gleaned from our own experiences and those of our students, as well as from the results of an exploratory research study conducted by one of the authors (Ertmer, Newby, & MacDougall, 1996).

▶ **There is no one right answer.** If you enter the case-learning experience with this idea firmly planted, you are less likely to be frustrated by the ambiguity inherent in the case-study approach. There are many answers to the issues in each case. The solutions you propose will depend as much on the perspective you take as on the issues you identify. Sometimes it may help to know how the designers in the cases "solved" the problems, but not always, and probably not usually. Being frustrated by a lack of answers can actually be very motivating. If you're left hanging after reading a case, chances are you'll continue to ponder the issues for a long time to come. As one reviewer noted, "After reading the first few cases, I felt that this is 'hard work' and it was going to take some time to work through— but they (the cases) made me stop and think about potential solutions. Some time after reading them I still found myself contemplating potential answers."

Accept the fact that you will not know how to solve each case. Furthermore, if you have no clue where to begin, give yourself permission not to know. Then begin the analysis process by paying attention to how others analyze the case based on their own personal experiences.

▶ **There is more than one way to look at things.** One of the advantages to participating in case discussions is that you get the chance to hear how others analyzed the case and to consider multiple points of view, thus gaining a more complete examination and understanding of the issues involved. Not only will listening to others' ideas *allow* you to see the issues from different points of view but it will also *force* you to consider exactly where you stand. By paying close attention to what others have to say, you can evaluate how that fits with your own views. Thus, you learn more about who you are, where you are coming from, and what you stand for. Your views of others, as well as of yourself, may be broadened.

▶ **Keep an open mind; suspend judgment until all ideas are considered.** This suggestion builds on the last. It is important to come to the case discussion with an attitude of, "Let's see what develops." Begin by regarding your initial solutions as tentative. Listen respectfully to your peers; ask questions to clarify and gather additional information, not to pass judgment on ideas different from yours. As one of our students recommended, "Be flexible and open-minded. Remember that problems can be attacked from many different angles." Use the case discussion as a means to gather additional data. In the end, your final recommendation should be informed by the collective wisdom of the whole class yet reflect your own best judgment.

▶ **Be leery of assumptions and generalizations; avoid seeing things in extremes.** If data are ambiguous or there is little evidence to support why case players acted as they did, be cautious of the assumptions you make. Be especially careful to state your assumptions tentatively, suggesting uncertainty. Along these same lines, be careful not to generalize your observations beyond the data provided. Avoid using labels or slogans that lump people together. If you're inclined to see things in black and white, all or nothing, stand back and look at the words you use in your analysis. It is fairly safe to say that you should avoid words such as *always, never, everybody,* or *nobody.* Stick close to the facts when describing the issues, drawing conclusions, and making recommendations.

▶ **Expect to get better; focus on the analysis process.** At the beginning of a case-based course, you may feel overwhelmed with the challenge of trying to solve case problems. It is important to recognize, first, that this is not uncommon. Many students initially feel overwhelmed and apprehensive. Second, it is equally important to recognize that, as with most skills, design skills and knowledge improve with practice. Furthermore, most students actually start to enjoy the challenge involved in analyzing problematic situations. If you maintain the mindset that you learn as much, if not more, from the analysis process as you do from identifying a potential solution, then your case-learning experience will be less frustrating. The analytic process is at the heart of the case method. Pay attention to the progress you make in analyzing the cases. Judge your success not by how many you "get right," but by your approach to the analysis process. Did you consider all the issues? Did you look at issues from the varying perspectives of the key players? Have you based suggestions on available data? If your skills are improving in these areas, you're gaining in precisely the ways promoted by the case approach. And remember that learning is a lifelong process. You'll never know all there is to know about designing. Yet each experience with design situations should move you closer to thinking and acting like a professional designer.

▶ **Take time to reflect.** Reflection has been a recurring theme in our discussion of how to approach a case study. Quite simply, that's because we believe that reflection enhances everything that happens in the case method. According to Rowland (1992), "Reflection is critical to understanding experiences and to developing skills. Students must engage in reflective conversations with themselves and with others in order to make sense of experience and deepen their understanding" (p. 38).

It's true that a case analysis takes more time to complete than traditional course assignments. Yet there is little to be gained by trying to rush the process. Acting or responding impulsively decreases the chances that you will gather all the relevant information, examine all the potential courses of action, and consider the many possible ensuing consequences. Take time to think. Ask questions of yourself, your peers, and your instructor. Hills and Gibson (cited in Grimmett & Erickson, 1988) describe how reflective practitioners might go about their work. The development of this type of reflective mindset can begin with your work on these cases:

> As you go about your work responding to phenomena, identifying problems, diagnosing problems, making normative judgments, developing

strategies, etc. think about your responses to situations and about what it is in the situation, and in yourself, that leads you to respond that way; think about the norms and values on which your judgments are based; think about the manner in which you frame problems, and think about "your conception of your role." "Surface" and criticize your implicit understandings. Construct and test your own theories. (p. 151)

▶ **Enjoy yourself.** As indicated earlier, the case method may at first feel like a strange and difficult way to learn. Yet, even when students indicate that learning from case studies can be frustrating and "unnerving," they also admit that it is exciting and valuable. Being actively involved, working with stimulating case material, having a chance to express your ideas and hear those of others—these are all enjoyable aspects of case learning. We think one of our students summed it up wonderfully: "I like how cases challenge you and frustrate you. My advice is to relax. Let the ideas flow. Don't say 'This isn't possible.' And, most of all, be confident that what you are doing now will pay off in the future." We echo these sentiments: Relax, enjoy, and get ready to learn!

REFERENCES

Boud, D., Keogh, R., & Walker, D. (Eds.). (1985). *Reflection: Turning experience into learning.* New York: Nichols.

Ertmer, P. A., Newby, T. J., & MacDougall, M. (1996). Students' approaches to learning from case-based instruction: The role of reflective self-regulation. *American Educational Research Journal, 33*(3), 719–752.

Grimmett, P. P., & Erickson, G. L. (1988). *Reflection in teacher education.* New York: Teachers College Press.

Kitchener, K. S., & King, P. M. (1990). The reflective judgment model: Ten years of research. In M. L. Commons, C. Arman, L. Kohlberg, F. A. Richards, T. A. Grotzer, & J. Sinnott (Eds.), *Adult development: (Vol. 2). Models and methods in the study of adolescent and adult thought* (pp. 63–78). New York: Praeger.

Noordhoff, K., & Kleinfeld, J. (1990). Shaping the rhetoric of reflection for multicultural settings. In R. T. Clift, W. R. Houston, & M. C. Pugach (Eds.), *Encouraging reflective practice in education: An analysis of issues and programs* (pp. 163–185). New York: Teachers College Press.

Rowland, G. (1992). What do instructional designers actually do? An initial investigation of expert practice. *Performance Improvement Quarterly, 5*(2), 65–86.

Shulman, L. (1992). Toward a pedagogy of cases. In J. H. Shulman (Ed.), *Case methods in teacher education* (pp. 1–30). New York: Teachers College Press.

Part II

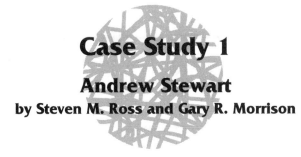

Case Study 1
Andrew Stewart
by Steven M. Ross and Gary R. Morrison

Dr. Andrew Stewart looked forward to his meeting on Tuesday with Dr. Lois Lakewood and her staff at Rainbow Design. Aside from wanting to see Albuquerque again (it had been about 10 years since he last visited), he viewed his assigned role, as "program evaluator," in Rainbow's design project as something he was not only well prepared to handle but would enjoy as well. Stewart was a professor of instructional design (ID) at a large university in Boston. He was knowledgeable about many aspects of design theory and practice and considered a national expert in educational evaluation.

For Stewart, the professional challenge and opportunity seemed tremendous. Rainbow Design had been awarded a $1 million contract from BTB Global Transport (a large and profitable shipping firm) to develop a user support system for a new computer system, called *Galaxy*, being developed for BTB. The new system would support nearly all business functions, such as inventory management, accounting, billing, and ordering, and would require substantial changes in employee job functions and specific tasks.

On Tuesday, Stewart arrived early at Logan Airport in an effort to escape some of the office distractions and to gain additional time to review Rainbow Design's plan of work. By the time the airplane boarded, he had become thoroughly reacquainted with the "meat" of the plan. Rainbow Design would need to develop varied types of user supports, using a learner-control-type format. Specifically, for each job task (e.g., accessing a customer's order number), the employee would be able to select online support when needed from a menu of options including, for example, cue cards (brief definitions, reminders, or directives), computer-based instruction (CBI), wizards (intelligent demonstration/application functions), and coaches (response-sensitive correction/feedback). Stewart's main responsibility would be to conduct a formative evaluation, first of the overall design approach, and later of the individual support tools as they were developed.

Engrossed in his reading, Stewart barely noticed the smooth take-off of the plane as it left Boston behind and cruised toward the West and Albuquerque. The effects of his early morning wake-up made him drowsy, but before allowing himself to drift off, he wanted to study one additional part of the plan—the staffing section. It looked good. Rainbow Design had a project manager, Cecilia Sullivan, who would perform necessary administrative functions but remain removed from ID decisions. Lois Lakewood, a talented and experienced designer with a doctorate from a nationally recognized graduate program, would head a diverse team of seven designers, including experts in text instruction, computer programming, CBI, and technical graphic design. In a vague, semiconscious way (especially in his sleepy state), Stewart experienced some discomfort with the role of a second, external design team housed in St. Louis. Because BTB Global Transport had a large satellite division in St. Louis, Sullivan thought it wise to hire local designers who could interface with the computer programmers in St. Louis to acquire better understanding of how the Galaxy computer system would work when completed. A formidable challenge in this project was that user support prototypes would need to be developed based solely on impressions and draft models of Galaxy—because the real system wouldn't exist for an indeterminate time. The St. Louis team consisted of three young designers, all having master's degrees in instructional design from Davis University in St. Louis. Their leader, Alicia Rosenthal, in her early thirties, was completing her dissertation for a doctoral degree there.

After arriving in Albuquerque, Stewart made good time while taxiing to the Rainbow Design office, which was located in a suburban strip mall about 10 miles from the airport. The meeting started as scheduled at 1:00 P.M. All the major participants were there, including the Rainbow team, the St. Louis team, and the BTB project manager, Carlton Grove. Lakewood did an excellent job briefing the group on the purposes of the project. Grove described his expectancies and displayed, despite the lack of much formal ID training (his background was human factors), an excellent intuitive grasp of how user support should be employed and how to increase attractiveness and utility.

Several times during the discussions, Stewart observed that the St. Louis team, through facial gestures and side comments, was inattentive and disapproving of the orientations being proposed. The team had prepared a set of detailed flow diagrams, which, according to their brief description, established a support selection model based on the works of Gagné, Mager, and other theorists. However, there was little time to study the selection model sufficiently, and, as Stewart observed, the St. Louis team members themselves had little interest in it since they appeared to be primarily a practitioner-oriented group. Lakewood, he noted, frowned in response to the antics of the St. Louis team, and, when speaking, seemed somewhat tense and guarded.

Stewart closed the day with a clear and forceful overview of his formative evaluation plan. He described it as involving progressive stages of increasing focus and comprehensiveness, as the support prototypes evolved from early drafts to near-final products. In all phases, the evaluation would include multiple data sources (different instruments from different participant groups) to provide triangulation and increase the amount of feedback regarding the quality of the design and its products.

Over the next two months, the Rainbow staff generated several user support prototypes for various employee job functions. Disappointingly, the St. Louis group, given the same assignment, was slow to produce any actual materials, and still seemed constrained by their strict adherence to "textbook" models they had studied in their ID courses.

In several conference calls between Stewart, Lakewood (Rainbow), Rosenthal (St. Louis), and Grove (BTB), there was obvious strain in the discussions. Provoked largely by Rosenthal's frequent resistance to the directions proposed, each stakeholder increasingly pursued an individual agenda for his or her team's work. Stewart's agenda, however, was already clearly defined by the current status of the project. With the first series of user supports developed and substantive costs already incurred (as Grove frequently reminded the group), it was time to initiate the formative evaluation. Grove wanted it done "yesterday," but "next week would be okay." Stewart mused that this was exactly the type of real-world situation he recently warned his graduate students to expect.

Over the next few days, Stewart drafted questions and rough instrument plans and faxed them to Lakewood, who turned them, almost magically it seemed, into a professional, polished set of materials. The final product was an "evaluation manual" consisting of a complete set of instructions, prompts, and instruments for guiding the evaluation step by step. In brief, the basic orientation, as designed by Stewart, was "one-on-one" trials in which each participant (interviewee) would: (1) describe his or her background and job activities; (2) "walk through" a simulation of a computer-based job function in the transportation industry (specifically, scheduling rail shipments); (3) examine sample user support tools made available for specific tasks; (4) rate each tool on various utility, user-interface, and aesthetic dimensions; (5) "reflect aloud" on its possible application; and (6) make recommendations. The manual was directly coordinated with the computer simulation and provided (so Stewart and Lakewood believed) tight control over the data collection process as well as an efficient data recording system.

The final steps before launching the evaluation were to arrange for interviews and to train the evaluators. Interviewees would be approximately 10 employees at 6 different national BTB sites. The evaluators would consist of mixtures of designers from Rainbow Design, and include, to a more limited extent, Stewart (given time and travel constraints) and St. Louis staff (given Lakewood's concerns about their commitment and orientation).

Three days before the first set of interviews were to take place, in the Minneapolis division, Lakewood received a call from Rosenthal, who said, "Given that we've been kind of impeded in our work with the BTB tech types here, I am very interested in taking a lead role in collecting evaluation data from the users. This would give me and my staff a real good feel for who's out there in BTB. User analysis is really our strength." Lakewood felt a tinge of anxiety about this proposal, but the idea did have some merit. It would occupy the St. Louis group (finally!); it would be good politics with her boss, Sullivan, who had hired the St. Louis team; and it would free the Rainbow staff, who now wouldn't have to travel as much, to work on the design task with their increasing demands. An agreement was reached whereby Rosenthal and staff would do the bulk of the user interviews (about 40 out of 60). They flew into Albuquerque, met with Stewart and Lakewood, and, along with the Rainbow crew, received training on the evaluation procedure.

Data collection began. Over the next few weeks (through the end of March), Stewart and Lakewood each administered a few interviews and felt good about the procedures and materials they had designed. Rosenthal called Lakewood intermittently to give status reports from the field (they were always positive). Grove from BTB called Stewart on April 2 to request that an evaluation report be submitted as a "deliverable" on April 15. "This can be done," Stewart thought, but he'd need Rosenthal to wrap things up in a week or so and get the data to him. Rosenthal, in a call to Lakewood, agreed.

On April 10, a large package with a St. Louis return address arrived at Stewart's Boston office. Stewart opened it with anticipation. He would now need to contact his graduate student assistants, who would code and analyze the data. Pulling the flaps of the box up, he immediately saw a cover memo from Rosenthal ("Here are all of our data forms—42 interviews!!"). He then removed a stack of about 10 evaluation manuals from the top. All seemed to have the top page correctly filled out—interview name, employee name, time, date, and so on. When he turned to the second page, he noticed that it wasn't filled out. There were no user ratings of the first support tool, only the evaluator's handwritten notes. The same was true for the rest of the manual—no ratings, only brief, often illegible comments. "Perhaps this one just didn't go right," he thought. "Really, can't use it." Looking at the next manual, his pulse increased, and then at the next manual and then two more, his heart raced even faster. He dug into the middle of the box and grabbed a stack of three manuals. Same thing. All were filled out in the same informal way that completely omitted the ratings!

It was the next day by the time his call to Lakewood produced the call to Rosenthal that brought Lakewood's call back to him—with the bad news. Rosenthal's group had decided on their own that the evaluation manual was really just a "heuristic" (general guide) and that the rating scales and specific comments weren't actually needed. "For doing user analysis," Rosenthal explained, "my designers favored a more holistic and qualitative orientation." Thus, they formed global opinions that they were certainly willing to share. (Stewart, too, had some opinions, but "share" would be too gentle a way to present them.)

The aftermath in the next few days was that Rosenthal and her group were severely reprimanded by Sullivan and put on "probation" in the project. But Stewart had a report to submit. Grove, from BTB with his scientific orientation in human factors research, would be expecting at least some quantitative results (bar charts and the like), and Stewart had only about 13 correctly completed evaluation manuals—the ones from himself and Rainbow Design. The report was due in three days.

Invoking ID practice via the Andrew Stewart case

1. Discuss each issue in the case from the perspective of the four key roles featured: evaluator, design manager, external design team, client project manager.

2. Evaluate the actions taken in the four key roles in terms of making the final product (the evaluation study) successful.

3. Discuss what actions you might have taken in each of the four roles to avoid the problems that occurred.

4. Create a scenario in which the final outcomes are satisfaction by each of the four key stakeholders and a successful evaluation study.

Case Study 2

Antonio Mendez
by Anna Flynn and Jim Klein

Julie Leung, principal of Master Elementary School, pushed her chair back from her desk, let out a sigh of frustration, and asked herself, "How am I supposed to bring this school up to date technologically when we can't even get Internet access?"

Leung, in conjunction with members of the School Improvement Team and the district's Technology Planning Committee (TPC), had just met to consider how to ensure that students and staff were technologically literate and made maximum use of technology (specifically the Internet) in their Master School Learning Community. One of the parent representatives on the School Improvement Team, a professor at the local university, offered to organize an instructional design (ID) team of doctoral students to meet with the principal and TPC to assess the school's technology needs and make a proposal to help the school meet one or more of its objectives. The ID team, led by Antonio Mendez, first visited the school in September.

▶ Master Elementary School Background

Master Elementary School is a K–5 public school located in Albuquerque, New Mexico, serving approximately 400 students with its 30 teachers and staff. The school had a computer lab consisting of 30 somewhat dated computers that were not linked to the Internet, and two computers with Internet connections that were located in teacher work areas. The school district allocated funds for computer hardware and software, but at the start of the project, Master Elementary had not yet received funding for upgrading equipment or providing Internet access from the computer laboratory. However, Leung was confident that the school would receive funding in the near future, and she wanted her teachers to be ready to use the technology as soon as it was available.

▶ Current Classroom Use of Technology

A preliminary survey of teachers revealed that each class spent 30 minutes twice a week in the computer lab. Other technology being used in the classroom included overhead projectors and VCRs. Most teachers expressed curiosity and interest in the Internet as a classroom tool, although hardware and software limitations prevented use of the Internet and e-mail in the computer lab.

Teacher Capabilities and Interests

As in most schools, the teachers, staff, and students differed in their knowledge and use of computers. The technological literacy of teachers at Master varied greatly from minimal knowledge, to use of word processing, to accessing NASA through the Internet. Most teachers expressed an interest in learning other ways to integrate emerging communications technology into their classes, but lack of time and inadequate technology were major hurdles to overcome. However, some teachers had computers at home and were knowledgeable and facile at navigating the World Wide Web to access classroom resources. Other teachers knew very little, and some had never been on the Web and did not know the basic procedures for navigating the Web.

Also, teachers from the different grades were concerned with finding computer and Internet resources specifically for their age group. For example, kindergarten teachers wanted to know what computer skills they should be teaching kindergartners, and teachers of children with special needs wondered if there were anything on the Internet that they could use with their students. A broader concern was how to prepare the students technologically for high school, college, and the work world. The existing skill levels and needs of each class of students appeared to vary greatly.

School Improvement Team and Technology Committee

The mission of the School Improvement Team, which consisted of several teachers and parents, was to identify areas needing improvement and to recommend an action plan to Leung. One area identified by the team was the use of technology at the school. The team developed a goal and four objectives related to technological literacy, which were given to the TPC to implement.

Goal: Students and staff are technologically literate and make maximum use of technology in the Master School Learning Community.

Objective 1: Students graduate from Master School with the ability to use a computer as a tool to express thoughts and ideas, to analyze data, and to communicate using interactive programs.

Objective 2:   Teachers are trained to teach their students to use technology to maximize student learning.

Objective 3:   Parents are involved in the technological education of their children.

Objective 4:   All staff are trained to maximum use of technology in the performance of their duties at Master School.

Both the School Improvement Team and the TPC wanted to take concrete action to improve the computer skills and knowledge of the teachers and staff so that they could integrate the computer, especially the Internet, into classroom activities and lesson plans. Only Master Elementary and one other school (out of the seven in the district) were still awaiting funding for Internet hookup. Leung and the committee members felt certain that funding for Internet hookup would be allocated in the near future. They believed that advance training would give teachers an advantage when the funding actually came through.

Despite the limitations of the existing computer hardware and software, the School Improvement Team and the TPC still wanted to maximize use of Master's existing resources and prepare teachers for the day when Master would have full capability to access resources through the Internet in the computer lab. The committees pondered how to best proceed.

Mendez's ID team also wondered what the best approach would be, given the technological limitations and existing time constraints. If training were the answer, only two dates were available for a teacher in-service: October 18 and January 10.

Invoking ID practice via the Antonio Mendez case

1. Identify information needed to conduct a thorough needs assessment.
2. Specify effective methods, instruments, and procedures for determining the technology needs of the teachers, students, and staff at Master Elementary.
3. Suggest potential means for meeting varying needs of teachers, students, and staff; discuss the advantages and limitations to each approach.
4. Consider the goal and four objectives developed by the School Improvement Team. Discuss challenges associated with implementing each objective. How would you prioritize these?

Case Study 3

Carrie Brackman
by John P. Campbell

Carrie Brackman is the president and owner of Performance Consultants Incorporated (PCI). The company was created five years ago after Brackman retired as the vice president for Human Resources of Mason Insurance. During her 25 years in Human Resources, she led the company in introducing computer-based training and electronic performance support systems. She is a strong believer in improving productivity through employee training, a centralized support network, and integration of the latest technologies.

Performance Consultants Incorporated has grown rapidly over the past few years. Brackman started as the sole employee of a company now employing over 20 full-time people. In addition the company supports a number of subcontractors and part-time employees. PCI has a number of small and medium-sized clients in Boston, New York, and Washington, D.C. Most of the contracts are fairly small and for short-term projects. Many projects focus on conducting needs assessments and developing classroom-training materials. PCI is refocusing its mission toward the development of electronic performance support systems (EPSS). The company hopes development of electronic performance support systems will provide a steady, long-term source of income to maintain company stability. PCI's largest client in terms of revenue and repeat business has been Mason Insurance—the former employer of the company's president.

Mason Insurance is a Fortune 500 company based in Boston. The company has offices in all 50 states and in over 800 cities. Mason Insurance specializes in automobile, renter's, and homeowner's insurance. During the past few years, Mason Insurance has revamped its claims processing system. The old system was based on a centralized mainframe and was becoming antiquated and unreliable. The current claims system operates using a distributed computing model with standard Intel-based machines. By using a distributed computing model, the company was able to off-load some of the processing that was handled by the mainframe and spread the burden among the current desktop machines. Mason Insurance invested hundreds of millions of dollars to upgrade the equipment and educate its staff on the new system.

The staff education consisted of two components. The first component focused on computer literacy skills. Mason Insurance hired a number of small firms located near its offices to provide this assistance. Employees were provided with basic computer training (e.g., using the mouse, customizing the operating system). The second component focused on the new claims processing software. EZ-Claim, the claims software vendor, provided training at ten regional offices as part of its contract for the systems upgrade. The complete program was implemented over a six-month timeframe.

After many months, Mason Insurance noticed a dramatic increase in claims errors and time of payment of claims. The company thought it was due to the employees not using the new software effectively. Many executives within the company believed that inadequate training was the source of the problems. Others believed that problems were due to technical shortcomings. Mason Insurance hired PCI to conduct an evaluation to identify the source of the problems and make a proposal for changes. Jim Thomas, president of Mason Insurance, specifically requested that Brackman take the lead on the project. Over a three-month period, she conducted a number of interviews with company executives, claims supervisors, claim clerks, and EZ-Claim staff.

Brackman first talked with Barbara Wright, a claims supervisor in the Boston office. Wright supervised a team of 12 full-time and part-time claims clerks. Over the past 15 years, she had worked her way up through the company. She was first hired as a part-time claims clerk, promoted to a full-time position, and three years ago was promoted to her current position as supervisor. Wright and Brackman have worked together on a number of previous projects and have built a good working relationship. Brackman started the meeting, "Barbara, you know I have been asked by Mason Insurance to identify the issues revolving around a dramatic increase in claims errors and time of payment of claims. What do you think is the problem? Is the company not providing enough time for people to become adjusted to the new system or is there a real problem here?" Wright responds, "From my seat, I think the company has a real problem with this new system. Mason Insurance has jumped into this new technology and is now completely over its head. I'm trying to keep my area afloat, but I'm swamped with questions from the clerks. My clerks are frustrated and continually calling me over with questions. However, with this new system, I'm not much help at times. The EZ-Claims staff provided claims supervisors with additional training above the clerk's course, but that was not enough. Many times my response to the clerks is to check the manual, but the manual is difficult to use. Even if you found the information you needed, you'd have to translate the very technical jargon."

Brackman asks, "So what type of questions are the clerks asking?"

Wright explains, "The questions vary quite a bit. Some of the confusion focuses on the new terminology used in the software. For example, our paperwork has three identification numbers: office number, policy number, and claim number. The software now asks for the information in one field. So it looks like XXXX-XXXXXXXXXX-XXXXXXXXXX. This has been very difficult to keep straight, especially since our policy and claim numbers each have 10 digits. I have found a number of simple data entry mistakes and the new software has caused many of these. I have a great set of clerks in my area. We never had such basic mistakes with the old system." Wright shows Brackman some typical data entry mistakes and explains how these mistakes can dramatically impact the resolution of a claim.

Wright continues, "The EZ-Claim's staff has not been much help. They are located in California and their technical support staff does not open until 9:00 in the morning—California time. That is noon here. So for any problem we have, we can't address it until after lunch. I don't know about EZ-Claims. Their software seems to have many capabilities, but their support has been terrible. I think Mason Insurance was convinced by the Management Information Systems (MIS) department to use this software, but no one ever asked me about our requirements." After lunch, Wright arranged a meeting with a number of claims clerks so Brackman could hear their side of the story.

Brackman met with seven claims clerks in the company cafeteria after lunch. She explained, "I've been hired by Mason Insurance to examine the increase in claims errors and time of payment." She was not able to get another word in.

The claims clerks were very hostile. Bob Miller, a claims clerk, said, "The claims errors are not our fault. Our unit had a wonderful record before the new system was installed. EZ-Claims has not provided us with enough training. They completely change the computer, software, and data fields without any input from us. They shove us in a room for a great one-day course on basic computer skills but only give us a four-hour course on using the new software. You can't expect us to learn a complete new system in four hours."

Jodi Sanke continued, "Then the company gives us one set of manuals for all of us. So any time we have problems, we have to get up from our desks and wade through the 12-volume set and hope to find the information."

Marti Blunk interrupted, "And the training was terrible. Bob's right, you can't expect us to learn a new system in four hours. We sat in a room and they lectured at us. We did not have many opportunities to try the new software until we were expected to input claims. The EZ-Claims person was a computer geek. He was talking in a whole different language and did not understand the insurance business."

Brackman talked with the claims clerks for over an hour. But she knows that to every story there are two sides. So she made arrangements to meet with the EZ-Claims product manager, Rosie Saguro.

Prior to flying to California, Brackman researched the background of EZ-Claims. EZ-Claims is a small company and was created four years ago when a number of programmers left Claims Pro to start their own company.

A few small insurance companies in the California area have adopted the EZ-Claims software, but Mason Insurance is the largest adopter to date. Since Claims Pro cut its prices, EZ-Claims has been struggling to maintain its market share. As Brackman continued her research, she found that PCI and EZ-Claims had a lot in common. Both were small companies struggling to survive and grow. Both have some smaller clients, but Mason Insurance is their biggest client. Each company is hoping its work with Mason Insurance will be the key to its future.

Brackman starts the meeting by explaining her purpose in making the trip to California. She continued, "So what is your view of the problems at Mason Insurance?"

Saguro began, "I have been overwhelmed by the calls from Mason Insurance. I understand they are very upset with their increase in claims errors, but these problems are not EZ-Claims' fault. Mason Insurance is trying to blame their problems on our software, but you'll find that the problem is in their corporate headquarters. Mason Insurance was not willing to spend the money needed for successful implementation of our product. They wanted to implement a brand-new system for as little money as possible. For example, we wanted to offer their employees a more extensive training session, but they were unwilling to pay for our time. Mason Insurance even went to other vendors to provide the computer basics section of our training. In our proposal, we provided numerous options for training and support. These options ranged from in-house training courses to maintenance and service agreements. Mason Insurance elected none of these options and settled for a basic four-hour introduction to our system."

Brackman inquired, "So what was included in your four-hour session?

Saguro explained, "We sent out our best programmers to provide the training. These guys know the system inside and out. They could have answered any question about our software."

Brackman interrupted, "Can you show me the training program presented to the employees of Mason Insurance?" She and Saguro went through the training materials in detail. The original training program proposed to Mason Insurance was 40 hours. Even if the 40 hours had been retained, most of the training was lecture based, with some hands-on exercises at the end of each day. Brackman found the training difficult to follow and disjointed. She inquired if EZ-Claims collect evaluation data from its training sessions. Saguro said they had collected some data, but the results were not as good as usual.

On the second day, Brackman asked about the field names on the entry screen. Saguro explained, "We have told Mason Insurance many times that the field names can be changed and reorganized. They had three choices when we signed the contract. First, Mason Insurance could have specified the look and feel of their system when they purchased the system. The initial cost of the software would have been greater, but their clerks would have an easier time. Second, if Mason Insurance had customized their software in the beginning, they could have signed up for a maintenance agreement. Under the maintenance agreement, EZ-Claims would do minor updating of the data entry screens. Finally, they could have purchased the developer's kit and had their Information Systems office do the modifications. Changing the field names is an easy matter, but Mason Insurance decided against sending someone to our developer training and purchasing the development toolkit. It takes someone with some database knowledge, but for $25,000, they would have a person equipped to do the work in-house. We would have done all of the changes for $200,000. In the end, Mason Insurance elected not to take any of these options. So we provided Mason Insurance with our basic software package." Brackman was given a demonstration of the developer's kit. It was amazing how easy it was to change the claims clerk's screens. Any of her people could do the work very easily. In addition to the basic changes to field names and screen layout, the tools were available to make the screen more pleasing to the user.

After a break, Saguro asked, "Would you like to see our new performance support system (PSS) we are beginning to build?" Brackman was enthusiastic about the opportunity. The new PSS was in its early stages of development. EZ-Claims was attempting to address the complaints of the large amount of text-based documentation. They were building a context-sensitive help similar to the latest word processing packages available. Saguro explained, "Our hope is to develop the performance system that would make the manuals obsolete and reduce the need for training. We tried to convince Mason Insurance to fund the development of the system, but they were not interested—always worrying about the bottom line. I think the PSS would solve many of their problems, and maybe you can change their mind." EZ-Claims was struggling to develop an intuitive interface. Brackman provided a number of suggestions that Saguro and Bob Allen, the lead programmer, found very useful. Brackman, Allen, and Saguro discussed some alternative strategies for organizing and accessing the information and how an instructional designer may be a great addition for the EZ-Claims staff. Saguro inquired, "Carrie, you seem to have a talent in developing these types of systems. Does your company develop performance support systems?" Brackman explained that PCI has developed some smaller systems and hoped to be doing more of this work.

When Brackman returned from California, she met with Jim Thomas, president of Mason Insurance. The two of them have been friends for many years. They developed a strong relationship of trust during Brackman's tenure with the company. Thomas asked, "So what have you found out so far? I need a proposal on my desk as soon as possible. The company is losing money every day we have these problems and in the long term, we may be losing customers."

Brackman responded, "I have interviewed a number of people within the company and at EZ-Claims. I have found a number of basic problems, but I still need some more time to build my recommendations."

Thomas interrupted, "I know you haven't had much time, but I need your proposal soon. I want a proposal with strong and specific recommendations. The recommendations need to include associated cost and your preferred vendor—even if that means your company. I can almost assure you that we will adopt most reasonable recommendations from your report in a timely fashion."

When Brackman returned to her office, she found an e-mail message from Saguro of EZ-Claims.

```
Subject: Your Visit
Date: Tue, 12 Aug 97 08:40:57 PST
From: rsaguro @ezclaims.com
To: cbrackman @pci.com

Carrie,
We really enjoyed your visit. Thank you for your
advice on our performance support system. Bob Miller
wants to hire your company to help on the PSS if we
get some additional funding. I would like to get your
company involved in our future training development.
Maybe we can develop a close alliance that will allow
both of our companies to succeed. Let me know how your
Mason Insurance proposal is going.

Take care,
-- rosie
```

Brackman returned to her notes and puzzled over how she should present her recommendations. Which potential solutions should she present and what vendors should she recommend?

Invoking ID practice via the Carrie Brackman case

1. Identify the major stakeholders in this case.
2. Identify specific ethical issues Brackman faces when developing a project proposal for Mason Insurance.
3. Identify whom Brackman can talk with about these ethical issues and their implications.
4. Discuss how Brackman can resolve these ethical issues. How might different solutions affect other stakeholders in the case?

Case Study 4

Clare Morris
by Joanna C. Dunlap

Clare Morris stared at the television screen shaking her head. Feeling an overwhelming need to verify what she had just seen, she rewound the videotape and pressed play again. There was no question about it. She made notes on her pad indicating what could be salvaged and what could not. Unfortunately, many of the segments would have to be reshot. Field shots at that! She tried not to think about how much time and money had been wasted. She also tried to control her anger... why hadn't Mark followed her directions? The content of that day's footage had been clearly defined, scripted, and storyboarded to avoid this very problem. She finished writing her notes, ejected the videotape, shut down the equipment, and walked out of the editing suite.

▶ Background

Morris is the instructional designer for Clarkstone University's distance learning program. Clarkstone's distance learning courses are designed to provide professional, working adults with a more convenient way of completing undergraduate and graduate degrees. All of Clarkstone's distance learning courses have an asynchronous broadcast/video component. Because Clarkstone does not have in-house video production facilities, Morris contracts video producers, equipment, and facilities from local television stations and video production houses. Her responsibilities include working with content experts to design the video content, scripting and storyboarding all video segments, and managing the overall production process.

Morris's first project at Clarkstone, nine months earlier, was a videotape component for a senior capstone course offered through Clarkstone University's distance learning programs in business administration, computer science, and elementary education. The video would present the requirements for a senior project, demonstrate the necessary steps, and provide real examples of senior capstone projects from three recent graduates—one from each major. The business administration graduate was a stockbroker whose senior project involved the development of an expert system that helped him create electronic portfolios for clients. The computer science student owned his own desktop publishing company and had developed a technical manual and web site for a client's new telecommunications product. The elementary education student was a third-grade elementary school teacher. For her senior project she developed a miniaturized model of the "perfect" classroom-based learning environment for young students—complete with teacher, students, furniture, and computer equipment—which she used to demonstrate how the classroom would be set up and used. After editing these segments and finalizing the other elements, Morris previewed the video and believed that she had accomplished the project's goal: to create a video that could be used by all three distance learning programs. However, when she showed it to an audience of Clarkstone program faculty, the associate dean jumped out of her chair and exclaimed, "We can't show this! It makes it look like men work on computers and women play with dolls!" Morris hadn't even seen the footage as potentially gender biased until that moment. To fix the problem, she interviewed another business administration student who had developed an electronic performance support system for her company and added the new segment to the video. It was a costly lesson, and Morris vowed to be more sensitive to how things can be interpreted, especially when they are committed to video.

Currently, among other things, she was working on the video courseware for an undergraduate accounting course that would be used by the business administration distance learning program. Because most of Clarkstone's business administration students were not planning to pursue careers in accounting, Morris, in consultation with the accounting faculty, decided to present the accounting material within the context of how project managers, marketing and sales managers, and operations/production managers use accounting information to make and support business decisions. By placing this information within these types of authentic activities, it was expected that it would be more relevant to the learners. Therefore, each lesson was designed to begin with a day in the life of a real company to illustrate how accounting information helps business people make day-to-day and long-term strategic decisions; the company would help establish instructional relevancy by showing students how accounting information is used to make business decisions in the real world. Real cases and scenarios would also take advantage of the strengths of the medium—realism, demonstration, gaining attention—and avoid the dreaded "talking head" mode of typical instructional video delivery.

Luckily, one of the accounting professors working on the project had a friend who owned a company called "The Gemstone Puppet Theater." The company, owned by successful entrepreneur Jill Boyd, designed custom-made individualized puppets for retail and ran a puppet theater with weekly performances. Boyd also took the puppet theater on the road, doing shows for schools, libraries, and special events. Her company had recently incorporated; a building was purchased to house the puppet theater, and five people had been hired to help with puppet designs and theater productions. This put Gemstone Puppet Theater in a perfect position to demonstrate how accounting information is used to make business decisions.

With the course content mapped out and the Gemstone Puppet Theater lined up, Morris needed to select the video producer and production facilities. The facilities were easy—she had established an ongoing partnership with one of the local public television stations and was always happy with their work. A producer was more difficult; she was currently working on multiple projects and really needed a producer who could work autonomously and follow her scripts and storyboards to the letter. When she told the station's production coordinator that she still hadn't lined up a producer, he recommended a well-known producer that had done a lot of documentary work for PBS. In fact, Mark Alexander had produced three award-winning documentaries for PBS, and his list of accomplishments filled Morris with confidence. And, as it turned out, Alexander was very interested in expanding his video production work into the educational market. Morris met with him right away and a contract was negotiated and signed.

During their initial planning meetings, Morris was struck by Alexander's enthusiasm and commitment to doing a good job. When she walked him through the scripts and storyboards for the video segments, he was forthcoming with video, graphic, and audio production techniques that would improve the video by gaining and holding viewers' attention and interest: animation, upbeat music, multiple cutaways, multiple camera angles, and humor. In awe of his accomplishments and extensive production experience, and in order to not stifle his enthusiasm or creativity, Morris neither agreed nor disagreed with his suggestions. Instead, she reiterated the importance of taking into consideration the demographics of the target audience (adult working professionals), the importance of the course content, and the need to portray the Gemstone Puppet Theater scenarios as authentically and professionally as possible.

On the first day of field shooting at the Gemstone Puppet Theater, Morris was scheduled to work on another project and therefore was not able to go on the field shoot with Alexander. So before her scheduled planning meeting with him the following morning, she went to the station to view the previous day's footage. Included with the waiting videotape was a note from him:

Clare -
The shoot went great! Jill and the rest of Puppet Theater staff were so easy to work with and the puppets really added a lot of splash to the shots. I'm really excited about getting your feedback on the work so far. I think this is some of my best work! I think you'll be really surprised at how well it's turned out. See you at 8:30!
- Mark

Morris inserted the videotape and pressed play. The introductory footage of Boyd and her staff at the theater looked great: it showed them working on a production line and building puppets, working on sets in the theater, and putting on a puppet show in front of a live audience. Next, Morris examined the footage of Boyd's various financial dilemmas, which highlighted how accounting information is used to help make good decisions. The first segment was supposed to show Boyd working on an inventory problem. Instead of showing her thinking aloud about how much it was costing her to stock various materials for puppet construction, she was shown conferring with Conroy the Coyote—one of her puppets! To top it off, the puppet was actually giving her advice! Although it was creative and made the scene more colorful, it was anything but professional or authentic; in fact, it took away from the authenticity of Boyd's inventory dilemma and nullified the reason for using a real company. It also made light of her dilemma and her company. Morris couldn't help but reflect on the similarities between Boyd getting financial advice from a puppet and the elementary education graduate "playing with dolls." Hoping that Conroy was only featured in this one scene, Morris fast forwarded through the rest of the tape. Unfortunately, Conroy played an active, advisory role in every scene. She reviewed the footage and took notes. Looking at her watch, she realized she had an hour to figure out how to clearly and constructively communicate her requirements to Alexander without interrupting the flow of production or bruising his creative ego.

Invoking ID practice via the Clare Morris case

1. Discuss the relationship between front-end analysis and instructional strategy selection.
2. Recommend appropriate instructional techniques for adult learners.
3. Identify appropriate instructional strategies when using video as an instructional medium.
4. Discuss the instructional value and limitations of using video to depict highly authentic settings and problem situations for instructional purposes.
5. Suggest strategies that an ID manager can use to optimize the quality of work produced by project developers.

Case Study 5

The COMET® Modules:
A Study in the Adoption and
Use of Learning Resources[1]
by Brent Wilson, May Lowry, and Joe Lamos

▶ The Interview

Brent Wilson and May Lowry stepped into Joe Lamos' corner office. Lamos is head of distance learning in the COMET Program. The COMET Program is a cooperative agency, funded principally by the National Weather Service with support from the Air Force and Navy, charged with linking forecasters with weather scientists through on-site and distance-based training programs. Lamos had stepped out, so Wilson and Lowry parked their bags and sat down at the roundtable beside Lamos' computer. Within a minute he arrived.

"Thank you for waiting." After pleasantries, Lamos initiated the conversation. "Let me give you some background. The COMET Program was started here in Boulder in 1989. UCAR—the University Center for Atmospheric Research—has a cooperative agreement with its sponsoring agencies to provide education and training in the application of the latest atmospheric science to weather forecasting. The program uses teams of university professors, scientists, working forecasters, and instructional designers to design a program to provide professional development to weather forecasters. This education and training both supports the modernization activities of the weather services and provides a resource for the larger meteorological community.

"The program we want evaluated is our DL Program—distance learning. The National Weather Service, Air Force, and Navy have about 5000 forecasters all over the world, including small local offices and overseas bases and ships. It is usually too expensive and time consuming to send those folks to a training center, so we are asked to provide on-station learning materials. What we have tried to do with the distance learning is to provide high-quality science information and forecast training, using state-of-the-art multimedia, first on videodisc and now on CD-ROM.

[1] The following case is based upon real events. The authors Brent, May, and Joe are playing themselves. The COMET Program is internationally recognized as a leader in weather training and performance support. The case is adapted from a summative evaluation of the COMET distance-learning program, conducted in 1995-96. The evaluation was based on site visits to 17 forecast offices; written questionnaires to selected forecast offices; focus-group interviews of forecast managers attending workshops and conferences; and analysis of extant reports, evaluations, and planning documents. While the overall case is based on actual events, details have been highly condensed, simplified, and changed to make the case suitable for instruction. The authors alone are responsible for any substantive errors or omissions.

"You've been contracted to evaluate our series of multimedia modules. We have nine modules out now, distributed to all forecaster offices in the National Weather Service, Air Force, and Navy. The modules run 4–12 hours in length and provide fairly comprehensive training on a variety of topics—forecast process, marine meteorology, and so on. After turning modules out for five years, we're ready for a comprehensive evaluation of their quality. We want you to find out how they're being received and used out in the field."

Lowry was listening intently. "Joe, tell us more about the module design."

"The modules are built around engaging scenarios depicting problems faced by forecasters," Lamos responded with enthusiasm. "Learners are encouraged to describe how they would approach the problem. They're provided with help in the form of information, advice, quizzes, animation, and video clips of experts discussing the particular weather topic and forecasting techniques. We've put a lot of work into our designs; they've won awards and we think they're generally very sound."

Wilson asked, "What leads you to look at evaluating the program now? Is there something in particular you're looking for?"

Lamos responded, "Our designers and staff meteorologists get out in the field occasionally. They're expected to write up and share a short trip report for every site visit they make. Lately these field reports have indicated a lack of use of the modules. We're hearing, word-of-mouth, that some offices don't have workstations operating correctly—or forecasters just aren't taking time to go through the material."

Lamos continued: "That's why you need to get out in the offices to see how forecasters are making use of the training. I also agree with you that a written survey will help you triangulate your office observations and interviews."

"It'll be loads of work, but I think it'll be worth it," Lowry agreed. "You don't do a comprehensive evaluation very often; best to do it right."

Lamos pulled out a summary sheet containing some key information about the COMET Program and the modules. "Here is the basic information you requested earlier in the week. I've tried to lay it out clearly and succinctly; ask me if you have further questions."

Brent took the sheet and glanced down the information. "Looks great, Joe. We'll take it from here."

COMET Program Summary Sheet

Mission. To provide training that shows forecasters how to apply the latest scientific findings to their everyday forecasting work.

Primary clients. Three government agencies: The National Weather Service (NWS), and the weather forecasting divisions of the Air Force

(AWS) and Navy (NMOC). There are more NWS personnel to train; they tend to have more formal education than Navy and Air Force forecasters.

COMET modules. Nine modules have been developed and disseminated to forecast offices. The modules are funded through a cooperative agreement between the COMET Program and its sponsoring government agencies and are automatically sent free of charge to all forecast offices. Each office has a COMET workstation, comprised of a videodisc player attached to a 386 or 486 computer.

Field support. The COMET Program has a telephone helpline that allows forecasters to call in with questions. Most questions have to do with setup and software problems. The workstations are supposed to be devoted to COMET modules, but many offices install other applications, causing occasional conflicts and bugs in the running of the modules.

▶ Field Interviews

Over a 30-day period, Wilson and Lowry traveled to various corners of the country, observing office conditions and interviewing forecasters. The following fieldnotes present essential findings of those visits.

Southland Air Force Base

Visitor: Wilson

The weather office is located within the main flight terminal building. The forecasting work area is directly connected to the pilot briefing area—not divided or separated in any way. Eight or nine forecasters are assigned to the office, with three or so on shift at a time. The COMET modules have been moved alongside a wall in the hall just outside the forecasting area, close to traffic between rooms. There seems little room to view the modules without being in the way of traffic.

STAN, Senior Airman.

The system keeps crashing. The main module that we use is for the Doppler radar. I just came out of school; I didn't know how to use Doppler. Pretty much that's what we use. The other modules are not used.

CELIA, Master Sergeant, Forecaster, 13 years forecast experience.

I did the Doppler series. It was interesting. They were good. To be honest, if I have to think about it I cannot remember any other ones that I've done. When I left here, COMET didn't work, but I guess it's working. About three quarters of the damn time it don't work. But Stan's in charge. Now we'll get it going.

How do we get trained? Around here, it seems like they just hand us new stuff to do, and it's kind of osmosis—I just learn to do it. You just pick everybody else's brain. Someone comes right out of school and says, "Hey, how come you're not using this?" So I learn how to use a new tool or database by picking other people's brains. We share ideas.

Westcoast Forecast Office, National Weather Service

Visitor: Lowry

The Westcoast Forecast Office is located in a beautiful new facility. Like the other NWS offices, the hub is a ring of computer workstations where the forecasters spend their time developing the weather products. This is a large office with 40 forecasters and interns and a large support staff.

▶ Group Interview

The group talked about the NWS as a "fair weather service"—that is, they operate on the premise that there will never be a weather emergency, no one will ever be out sick or take a vacation, so there is no slack at all in the staffing. This is a problem for training, because you have to pull someone off their shift, which they are loath to do. "Our ethic is that you shouldn't leave your station. You must maintain a presence at your desk."

MARK, the training officer.

Training is something you do continuously. It does not fit for us to go down the hall and around the corner and carve out time for a module. Training for a forecaster is apprenticeship, and the problem always is a lack of time. Forecasters are individually trained—OTJ.

Others in the group agreed that there wasn't enough of Mark to go around. A big help would be for the COMET Program to help Mark.

On the modules:

▶ Advantages: they are self-paced, you can go back to get information if you are reticent to ask someone in the office.

▶ Hardware is not sufficient.

▶ We need relatively small and discrete chunks (30–50 minutes).

▶ We really need instantaneous training on essential information.

▶ Shorter chunks: "We would love to have an hour on icing, an hour on turbulence, and so on."

▶ Make them application based—something they can use.

"COMET can help us best by helping us take local information and frame it so that we can use it to train our own." They gave the example of the 1986 flood in their area: "It is an important weather event to us, and we have knowledge of it in our heads. How can we best use it to teach our forecasters? We need an electronic three-ring binder."

Old Town Air Force Base

Visitor: Wilson

The forecasting office is located in one of the hangars near the air field, presently used by a fleet of vehicles. The office appears to be in serious need of remodeling. A divider separates the forecast area from the briefing area. When a pilot comes in for a briefing, the forecaster leaves the forecast area, walks around the divider, and offers the briefing.

A total of five forecasters are available for shift scheduling at this office. That averages about one forecaster in the office at any given time. Professional interactions are usually limited to shift changes.

PETE, Master Sgt., Station Chief/Superintendent, 12 years forecast experience.

We all know there's something in the modules to listen to, it's just different than what our focus is. We have never had the luxury of really forecasting the weather. What we've had to do is put together a forecast usually as fast as you can. You're talking to airborne air crews, and it's real easy to get into a reactive mode. You make the forecast quickly. An hour later your forecast is already blown. It doesn't take much for things to go to hell quick. . . what happens is we have to issue amendments. We have to answer telephones, issue briefings, deal with a number of clients at once, you don't really have time to do a thorough analysis like you'd like to do. If it was just forecasting, we could do a better job.

South River Office, National Weather Service

Visitor: Wilson

About a half-dozen forecasters are working. The COMET workstation is in the main room, partially partitioned yet close to the circular forecasting area. I observe a good amount of collaboration in the office, with forecasters occasionally consulting together.

JIM, Forecaster, 18 years forecast experience.

I like being able to move around and interact with the material. I like the practices on the material. You're able to learn that way. The material is good, good techniques.

An index would be useful for the modules. That way, let's say I'm dealing with a recurring situation here that doesn't seem to fit any model. I could try and look up similar cases in the modules, or look for ideas that might also account for what's happening. I'd also like an opportunity to raise some of these problems to the scientists, and get them to help us.

BLAIR, Lead Forecaster, 25 years forecast experience.

The location of the COMET workstation is separate from the work area. It's physically inconvenient for me to be walking over to the COMET workstation, work a few minutes, then have to go back to answer a phone. I feel disconnected over there. I get an extra shift about once every two to three months where I can work on a COMET module.

PAT, steward of the local union, 33 years forecast experience.

(On requiring completion of the modules.) It's tough to get too regimental in an operational environment. You can't dictate requirements because you have to allow people to be fairly flexible in doing their jobs.

From a union perspective, you probably could encourage individuals to complete certain modules, as part of their performance appraisals—you would want to negotiate that with them. But I don't think it would work as a national policy. I'm sure a national policy like that would require some kind of union approval.

Windy Point Office, National Weather Service

Visitor: Lowry

The Windy Point office is located in a somewhat remote area near the water with a view of the mountains. The heart of the office is a ring of computer stations. The middle of the ring is a work area with phones and rows of three-ring binders and other kinds of well-thumbed notebooks. Around the perimeter of the office are smaller cubicles for the forecasters and support people, a conference/training room, break room, storage rooms, and a cubicle devoted to the COMET workstation.

I arrived during a shift change. It reminded me of shift changes in hospitals during morning report or night report. The shifts overlapped so that the departing forecaster could brief the arriving forecaster. The weather had been quite mild, but the forecasters still took about 30 minutes to exchange information.

In addition to the formal briefing at the change of shift, I was struck by the amount of informal talk and exchange. It seemed that everyone was talking to someone else most of the time. Forecasters would sit at a station for a few minutes but would inevitably call someone over to look at the screen or would go over to another forecaster's station to compare notes. The norm seems to be collaboration with others and coordination of the work almost constantly.

Later, when I asked them about this coordination, the marine forecaster told me that no "weather product" goes out of the office without several people checking it and concurring. In addition, the marine forecast must be compatible with the public forecast and the aviation forecast, so that the office forecasts are consistent. Several people reminded me that forecasting is inexact, and two good forecasters can look at the same data and come up with different conclusions. They have to come to some consensus before the forecast goes public.

▶ Group Interview

▶ Give us something we can use at our workstations.

▶ Smaller topics! (enthusiastic agreement all around). We have two hours to look at modules on a really good day. Thirty minutes to one-hour chunks would be best.

▶ The index is missing; include a guide in the modules called "Dr. Raindrop" (office joke).

▶ Give a time estimate on each section so that we can plan when to use it.

▶ Give me something I can finish, otherwise I tend to go to sleep.

▶ Want something we can pull up—just in time—when we need it.

▶ A good source of information. I like the self-paced strategy.

JACK, Lead Forecaster.

Jack came on a later shift and wasn't there for the group interview. Nevertheless, the same themes came up in my conversation with him. Jack seems to be the grand old man of the office and everyone's mentor. Several people interrupted our conversation with questions for him. This seems to be the norm in the forecast office—more examples of collaboration in forecasting and the apprenticeship style of training in the office.

One of Jack's main jobs is coaching. He spends about 30 to 45 minutes "on the fly" with a forecaster. His materials are in binders he has collected over the years, including materials from COMET classes, which he thinks are great. He grabbed a binder and enthusiastically flipped through it. He said that every trainer has a binder like that full of their favorite maps, handouts, and so on. It is their personal cache, and they refer to them all the time—"the most useful training tool."

▶ Results of The Written Survey

The findings from the survey were mostly consistent with reports from site visits, focus groups, and interviews. The modules generally had a good word-of-mouth reputation among both users and potential users, but a low rate of use.

Module Use

Forecasters were asked which of the nine modules they had used or completed. Module use followed a distinct trend, with older modules used more heavily than newer modules. This declining use rate partly reflects less opportunity by the forecasters to review the modules. Use rates by the NWS are substantially higher than for either Air Force or Navy.

Module Design

The survey asked forecasters to rate the modules on appropriateness of content and effectiveness of instructional strategies and media. Overall, forecasters reported that the modules were well designed. They especially appreciated the multimedia format, interactive instructional strategies, and the fact that the learning was self-paced. Eighty-one percent reported that the COMET modules contained information that was useful to them in their jobs. A quarter of them felt that there was too much emphasis on scientific information and not enough on the everyday skills of forecasting. The most frequent complaint was not having enough time to complete the modules.

▶ Pulling it all Together

After four months of gathering information, it was time to make some sense of it. It was clear that the forecasters approved of the module design and sometimes used the modules, but that they were not getting full use out of them. Why not?

Wilson and Lowry knew that there were issues of time, hardware/software, relevance to the job, accessibility, and compatibility with the routines of work and training. Now it was time to formulate recommendations and help the COMET Program decide its course of action.

Invoking ID practice via the COMET Modules case

1. Review the codes we used for categorizing the evaluation data, reflecting factors that seemed to have some effect on the use rate of the modules:

    T . . . . . . time issues
    S/H . . . software/hardware issues
    R . . . . . relevancy to the work of the forecaster
    A . . . . . accessibility: Could the forecasters get to the modules to use? Once they got to them, could they successfully navigate inside the lesson?
    C . . . . . . compatibility: Do the modules fit with the work and training routines of the office?

2. Now that you have read our notes, would you add other codes to the list above? Would you modify or delete any? Provide a rationale for your decision.

3. Make a list of barriers to successful use of the modules. Which of these barriers seem most important—or are they all important? Develop a conceptual scheme for organizing these barriers into a meaningful framework (e.g., individual vs. group factors; motivational vs. information; performance context vs. training context). This conceptual scheme should prove useful in understanding the problem and developing appropriate interventions.

4. List some possible interventions or changes that would address the identified barriers. Classify interventions in terms of cost (expensive vs. inexpensive) and time (short-term or long-term).

5. Consider the value implications of various interventions. How radical should interventions be? For example, one intervention might be to rethink the COMET program's fundamental mission, emphasizing work performance over applying scientific knowledge. Such a change may have far-reaching consequences for the organization, including some unforeseen negative consequences. How do you decide a best approach?

6. Develop a set of recommendations to present to Lamos and the COMET program's staff for improving the effective use of the modules in the field. Be prepared to defend your recommendations with data and reasoning that links your recommendations to likely improvements.

Case Study 6
Denny Clifford
by Peggy A. Ertmer and Katherine S. Cennamo

Denny Clifford, an independent instructional design (ID) consultant, had never felt so bewildered—Dr. Cynthia Oakes was one of the most complex clients he had ever worked for! Clifford wasn't sure if this was due to the differences in their ages, gender, or educational experiences, or simply due to the nature of the project, but he found himself completely incapable of carrying on a meaningful conversation with Oakes. They just didn't seem to speak the same language!

Clifford was an experienced design consultant—he had worked for a video production firm for the last five years and was an Air Force technical designer/trainer prior to that. He had created a wide variety of instructional materials, including computer-based lessons, multimedia simulations, and distance education courses. Although Oakes had personally requested his help with the development of a set of innovative materials for middle school science teachers, this was the most difficult job he had ever accepted. Originally, he had thought that his basic understanding of science and technology would be a distinct advantage compared to other projects he had worked on; now he wasn't so sure. Maybe if he understood a little bit more about Oakes' teaching philosophy he wouldn't be so confused.

Oakes, a professor of science education at the local university, believed wholeheartedly in the constructivist approach to teaching and learning. Clifford learned, early on, that this translated into an aversion to such words as *objectives, criterion-referenced test items, directed instruction,* and *right answers.* Still, Oakes had requested Clifford's assistance in creating some instructional materials to help local middle school teachers teach in a manner consistent with science reform initiatives.

As in most middle schools, students at the local school change classes for instruction in various content areas; thus certain teachers are responsible for teaching science to multiple groups of students each day. Although some of these teachers have a real interest in science, most are simply assigned to teach science without much training or interest in the topic. Several years ago, Oakes received a large grant to develop science materials for this group of teachers.

As a national leader in the area of science education, Oakes developed an innovative curriculum based on a social constructivist view of learning. Quite simply, the curriculum consisted of a set of "problems" for students to solve. Oakes introduced the curriculum in local workshops where she explained her constructivist philosophy and provided an overview of the materials. The curriculum was wildly popular, leading to multiple requests from other school districts for Oakes to present workshops and inservices at their locality.

Now, Oakes has received a large grant to develop professional development materials for this audience. Money does not seem to be a concern; however, she has introduced a number of constraints to the project.

First, Oakes indicated that the purpose of this project was to help middle school science teachers: (1) generate multiple ideas from their students about how to solve a scientific problem, (2) listen to and make sense of the students' ideas about science, and (3) know what to do with these ideas (i.e., respond in ways that valued the students' ideas and provided opportunities for them to explicate their problem-solving strategies). Oakes didn't really care what specific content from the science curriculum Clifford focused on; instead, she wanted the teachers to learn an alternative way of teaching science to middle school students—that was the content she was most interested in teaching! In fact, she wasn't interested in *teaching* her content at all. She simply wanted to provide opportunities for teachers to "explore issues related to reform-based science teaching" in a "socially supportive" environment.

Second, Oakes believed deeply in the effectiveness of her approach to developing scientific reasoning. From earlier discussions, Clifford learned that science lessons typically began with pairs of students working on a problem from the curriculum and ended with them sharing their problem-solving strategies and solutions with the whole class in a large-group discussion. It didn't matter to Oakes if the middle school students gave the right answers to the problems; her interest was in developing the problem-solving *process*, not achieving particular learning outcomes in terms of content. In fact, she mentioned that there *were* no absolute right answers, since "all knowledge is socially constructed." And she wanted teachers to develop their pedagogical knowledge of science teaching in a similar manner.

Third, Oakes was particularly sensitive to her participants' needs. She was well aware that classroom teachers were extremely busy people. She was hoping to provide instruction in a format that allowed teachers to work on their own time, possibly at school or home. Of course, she expected that teachers would start utilizing innovative approaches to science instruction in their own classrooms.

Fourth, Oakes didn't have the time, or the desire, to conduct a series of inservices or workshops for the local teachers. She had done this a number of times over the past few years and was no longer interested in continuing in this vein. Her main interest was research. She was deeply interested in the effects of the curriculum on students' scientific thinking.

Typically, she provided extensive follow-up for each teacher who participated in her workshops. She observed their classes weekly and followed
these with individual meetings in which she discussed her observations.
In fact, she had published numerous articles in which she discussed children's learning in her problem-centered science curriculum.

It seemed to Clifford that Oakes was willing to find a way to meet the
need for the workshops but wasn't interested in delivering them. In fact, it
seemed that she had not really thought much about how to "package"
the instruction. Clifford wondered if much of her previous "instruction" on
the curriculum had occurred during one-on-one meetings with the
teachers. Although she did not want to spend her time conducting workshops, Oakes indicated that she was willing to meet with teachers for an
occasional half day to "share experiences and stories." But of course,
that would be impossible if the program were eventually distributed
nationally, as she envisioned. With the large number of requests for workshops, Oakes just didn't have time to do it all. That's why she contacted
Clifford—to design some other way to distribute the information.

At Clifford's last meeting with Oakes, she made it quite clear that she
expected him to provide a list of suggestions regarding his proposed
materials and delivery method at their next meeting, scheduled within a
week's time. Yet, to date, Clifford hasn't completed *any* of his normal ID
tasks. For example, he hasn't been able to develop a list of objectives or
assessment instruments. He has no specific content to work with; Oakes
seems to be the only subject matter expert available; in fact, he doesn't
even have a list of learner characteristics. Despite having had four meetings with Oakes, Clifford hasn't been able to obtain the information that
he normally gets from clients at the start of a project.

On reflection, however, Clifford realized that the following possible
resources, mentioned in conversations with Oakes, may provide him with
some direction, or at least a starting point:

▶ A list of 24 teachers who had completed the workshops in previous
  years. Many of these people were teaching in local schools and, for
  the most part, were still practicing the techniques they had learned.

▶ A box of videotapes, labeled by observation date, of these
  teachers in their classrooms as they were gaining experience
  with this approach.

▶ A copy of the grant proposal that funded the development of the
  materials for teachers.

▶ A list of local teachers who expressed interest in learning to teach
  science in a new way.

▶ A couple of articles that had been written by both Oakes and a
  former participant who was entering her fifth year of teaching science in a manner advocated by Oakes.

He does have his notes (see Figure 6.1) from these meetings and the
resources provided by Oakes, but the information still seems only remotely

Figure 6.1 Clifford's Notes from Meetings with Oakes

- Group discussions are important to allow opportunities for kids to create shared meaning of scientific ideas.
- Productive discussions allow kids to develop their scientific reasoning, to articulate their ideas, and to reflect on their reasoning and the reasoning of others.
- Teachers need assistance in becoming good discussion facilitators.
- Teachers need continual support while in the process of changing their practice.
- The teacher's role is critical in fostering students' ability to develop skills in scientific reasoning.
- Teaching in a manner consistent with reform initiatives requires a shift away from traditional teaching and a change in teacher practice.
- Change in practice is especially important in terms of conducting successful class discussions during science, which are critical to the success of this approach.
- Teachers lack the time and social support necessary to reflect on their practice.
- Materials are targeted for both new and experienced teachers, reinforcing teaching in a manner consistent with reform initiatives in science education.
- Participants should have already accepted the need for a learner-centered practice.
- Participants enroll voluntarily, so they usually have a positive attitude toward developing their practice. May have some anxiety about trying something new. Important to create trust and a nonjudgmental environment.
- Want participants to reflect on classroom practices of their own and others, and to develop action plans for continual development of practice.

related to his assignment. How is he going to deliver effective instruction when he can't seem to begin designing it?

Invoking ID practice via the Denny Clifford case

1. Describe the communication barriers operating in this case. Suggest strategies for circumventing or eliminating those barriers.
2. Describe how the identified resources can be re-purposed to address specific ID needs.
3. Recommend appropriate media, delivery mode, and instructional strategies for meeting the specific needs of a widely dispersed target audience. Justify your recommendations.
4. Draft an instructional strategy for a sample lesson that introduces these teachers to a constructivist approach to science teaching.
5. Suggest strategies to facilitate a mutually beneficial relationship between people with behavioral and constructivist points of view.

Case Study 7
Elizabeth Kirk
by Molly H. Baker

As director of the faculty support office on campus, Dr. Elizabeth Kirk had several opportunities to work with faculty interested in designing and developing technology-based products for use in their classes. In most cases, the faculty had served as subject matter experts (SMEs) who provided the core content for the product, but who preferred that Kirk's office take the lead on the creative, design elements of the projects. A number of resource personnel were available to Kirk to assist with the artwork and production, including Oystein Eftedal, a specialist in video and multimedia interface development. Since the faculty projects so far had been relatively limited in scope, and the faculty had welcomed significant guidance from her office, an informal working style had been established between her office and the production staff.

Dr. Thomas Mowen was a professor with 10 years of college teaching experience. In recent years, he had been very successful in securing grant money to fund curriculum development projects for K–12 math education and considered himself an expert in this area. His most recent undertaking funded the development of four videotapes and accompanying teacher guides for a middle school mathematics unit. He served as the SME for this project, working closely with a video production crew. About four months prior to the end of the funding cycle, he ascertained that he had sufficient dollars remaining to attempt a CD-ROM, the type of technology-based project he had been hoping to do to make his next grant proposal more attractive to the funding agency. Meanwhile, he signed a contract to market the video series through a catalog that targets K–12 teachers and curriculum directors.

Mowen contacted Kirk about helping him develop a CD-ROM to supplement the video series he had recently completed. Although he did not know her well, he had participated in several workshops that she had conducted for faculty and viewed a CD-ROM that her office had helped develop for one of his colleagues in another department. He felt confident that she could assist him in this project. They agreed to meet the following day to discuss his preliminary ideas.

Kirk found Mowen's enthusiasm contagious and his experience working with support staff on other projects a refreshing change of pace for her. He appeared to have lots of ideas, sufficient funds to hire Eftedal and a graphic artist, and a desire to be more closely involved with the CD-ROM design and development than many of her earlier clients. Eftedal was winding up another project, so would be able to devote time to this venture within a few weeks. Kirk, Mowen, and Eftedal agreed to meet the following Tuesday to begin the planning process; in the meantime, Kirk asked Mowen if he could provide her and Eftedal with a copy of the video series and support materials to review.

Tuesday's meeting proved to be a fruitful review of the video series package; however, when the discussion turned to the CD-ROM, the water became muddier instantly. Mowen felt that it was important to his future as a grant writer to get experience developing a CD-ROM, but he had given little thought to how it might contribute to the value of the curriculum package itself. Most of the meeting was spent exploring various options about:

▶ The CD-ROM audience (e.g., middle school learners, teachers, curriculum directors)
▶ The computer platform limitations that might be expected where the CD-ROMs would be utilized
▶ The purpose of the CD-ROM (e.g., stand-alone instruction on the same topic as the video series, supplementary instruction to the video series for teachers only, an introduction for marketing the video series)

Keeping the relatively short time frame and financial constraints of the project in mind, Kirk suggested that Mowen think about the options for a few days and then meet again with the team to make some final decisions. Eftedal asked Kirk later if he could be left out of the process until more planning was completed since he was busy finishing another project and felt Mowen was still very unfocused about the direction he wanted the project to take. Kirk agreed.

Friday, she and Mowen met for lunch. He had given the project a lot of thought, he said, and decided that he wanted the content of the CD-ROM to serve as a marketing tool for the video series as well as an instructional supplement for the middle school students. Kirk attempted to tactfully point out how difficult this would be since the audience, purpose, and distribution method were so very different for the two purposes, and there simply was not enough time or money to accomplish both objectives. She explained the differences between the two and attempted to guide Mowen toward making a decision to do one or the other. He reluctantly agreed and chose the "marketing" direction. At this point, Kirk suggested that he might want to contact the video production crew director to see if she would be available to cut some video clips for any potential sections that would feature the various videos in the series. Kirk also recommended that both of them review the tapes and supplementary materials again and think about potential content elements of the "marketing CD-ROM." They agreed to meet the following week to nail down the key sections, and then contact Eftedal to begin planning the "look" and "feel" of the interface design.

Over the weekend, Kirk worked on three versions of a content matrix. Each version included many of the same potential elements but placed the emphasis on different marketing messages:

▶ Taste-its of the video series

▶ Taste-its of the supplementary materials for teachers

▶ Sample lessons for integrating portions of the videos into existing math curricular themes for middle school math education

Kirk also sent an e-mail to Mowen (and Eftedal) with a brief description of the three potential emphases, suggesting that Mowen might want to think about which of these plans he felt would generate the most interest in the video series among members of the target audience (teachers and/or curriculum directors). She also mentioned that if he had other suggestions for a different approach, that would be wonderful. These were simply ideas to give the content analysis phase of the project a jump start. Privately, Kirk also e-mailed Eftedal that she and Mowen would probably be contacting him about a "meeting of the minds" conference within the next week or so to begin the process of interface design. Perhaps the copy of her memo to Mowen would give him a chance to begin thinking about possibilities, she said. Also, did he still think the remaining time frame was realistic? Would it speed up the process to make contacts for subcontracting graphic design and video clip digitizing now? If so, did he want to do that or should she?

The following week, Mowen and Kirk met in her office. Kirk had generated copies of possible flowcharts representing the three content matrices. Mowen brought a list of potential topics/elements to include on the CD-ROM. His list included some of the marketing elements that appeared on Kirk's flowcharts, and lots of elements for an instructional section for the middle school students. Kirk expressed surprise that he had worked on the latter when she thought they had agreed that the two-part approach had been abandoned last week in favor of the marketing emphasis. Mowen firmly stated that he felt confident Eftedal could help them find a way to do both. The remainder of the meeting was spent discussing the pros and cons of such an approach (pros from Mowen's perspective, cons from Kirk's) and what message they would relay to Eftedal at the meeting with him later in the afternoon. Eventually, Mowen agreed to return to the marketing emphasis. However, there was no time to select which marketing approach to adopt, so they agreed to discuss this with Eftedal later in the day.

By afternoon, Kirk had e-mailed Eftedal to warn him of Mowen's wavering commitment to a single focus. Eftedal notified Kirk that he had invited the video series production director and a graphic artist to attend the meeting to assist with any brainstorming of interface ideas and share any technical limitations of the CD-ROM. He wondered if he should cancel these arrangements given the "less-than-firm" direction the project was taking. Kirk responded that they should come. Perhaps the collective opinion of all of them about the importance of a single focus would help Mowen see the value in proceeding with the project as conceived last week.

Fortunately, the afternoon meeting went well. Mowen and the other team members successfully reviewed the various marketing approaches proposed by Kirk, selected the one that emphasized the taste-its of the video series (with one sample lesson using clips from the series), and brainstormed ideas for interface design. The group also worked out a tentative timeline for the next month that included graphic and video work by the production crew and more detailed content analysis work by Kirk and Mowen.

Over the next month, all parties worked to produce their various components. Kirk and Mowen worked on more detailed flowcharts for each section. Mowen appeared settled with the direction the project was going, and enjoyed working on selecting the various video clips that he wanted to have digitized for the taste-it sections. Near the end of the month, Eftedal informed Kirk that the graphic artist was ready to share a "mock-up" of the interface, and Kirk indicated that she and Mowen were ready to discuss the content prescriptions for each section. All agreed to meet in the lab where the interface could be viewed on a computer screen similar to ones owned by the target audience. To everyone's surprise, Mowen didn't like the "dark" interface and again tried to argue for a button that the users could click that would take them to an instructional section. Once again, Kirk tried to explain why a single approach was needed. The production staff listened tactfully, and Mowen left early for another meeting. Kirk felt as if they were back at square one. What should she do now?

Invoking ID practice via the Elizabeth Kirk case

1. What are the major problems in this situation from Kirk's point of view?
2. Describe how the desire for changes during the content analysis phase might be better handled.
3. Recommend how to distribute responsibilities among team members to achieve efficient management of the CD-ROM project.
4. Suggest a communication structure to implement the recommendations made in response to the previous question.
5. Evaluate Kirk's performance as an instructional design consultant. What advice would you give her at this point as to how to proceed with the project?

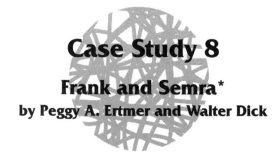

Case Study 8

Frank and Semra*
by Peggy A. Ertmer and Walter Dick

In 1989, the government of a Southeast Asian country (referred to here as (SEA), in cooperation with a major U.S. electronics corporation, began to plan the development of a training design center in SEA in which participants would be trained to design instruction using the systems approach. The hope was that SEA would obtain the long-term capability to determine the need for, and then to develop, appropriate training programs for its workforce. At the time this decision was made, there were no instructional design (ID) training programs being offered in SEA, although there were various training institutes in operation (e.g., the Teacher Training Institute, the National Training Center, and the Vocational Education Center) and numerous government employees who provided training for local businesses. So although these employees served as trainers, they themselves had received little, if any, formal instruction in design theory or practice, and furthermore, they had never participated in a curriculum that employed a systems approach to the design and development of training. Although SEA trainers often delivered instruction on specified content, they had no formal experience with, or knowledge of, adult learning principles or the use of interactive teaching strategies. The instruction they created typically depended on their own content expertise or revolved around instruction that had been imported from the United States and then adapted.

A pair of U.S. designers was hired to plan and develop a curriculum for preparing SEA instructional designers. One of these designers, Frank Tawl, was a university professor and a noted expert on the use of the systems approach for designing instruction. Frank had developed a number of courses at his U.S. university that related to ID topics and issues and felt fairly confident that these could be modified to fit the SEA learners' needs. Tawl's teammate, Semra Zusnis, was a private consultant who had worked with Tawl on a number of previous projects and was noted for her ability to

*Based in part on a 1991 article by Walter Dick that appeared in *Performance Improvement Quarterly, 4*(1), "The Singapore project: A case study in instructional design," pp. 14–22. Used with permission of the author and publisher. Note that information from the original case was altered in order to increase its educational value for our readers. Readers should not consider this case to be a true representation of the Singapore government.

recognize and address culturally relevant issues in situations involving learners from diverse backgrounds. As part of their front-end analysis, Tawl and Zusnis conducted interviews to determine the current perceptions of professors at the national university, as well as training staffs at the Teacher Training Institute, National Training Center, and the Vocational Education Center, regarding the proposed ID training curriculum. Among other things, they were interested in determining: What kind of training experiences were currently in place at the existing training centers? What procedures did SEA trainers follow when designing and presenting new instruction to fellow Asians?

In these initial interviews it became clear that the professors at the national university were supportive of whatever the Americans thought best—teaching whatever content Tawl and Zusnis thought was appropriate, as well as using whatever strategies the Americans typically used. During follow-up interviews they posed virtually no opposition to Tawl's and Zusnis's ideas; after a suggestion was made, the professors would simply nod in agreement. Although Tawl and Zusnis made a concerted effort to uncover any culturally sensitive issues that should be taken into consideration in the design of the curriculum, they identified almost none. If the SEA professors had any culturally related concerns, they didn't acknowledge them.

Additional interviews were held with potential students for the ID curriculum, namely, the current trainers. Tawl and Zusnis asked questions to determine the following: What did the SEA trainers already know about the design process? What beliefs did they hold that reflected possible acceptance of the systems approach and/or findings from current research regarding the teaching/learning process? What beliefs seemed contradictory to these current theories about teaching and learning? How motivated were they to participate in this new training program? Although, on the surface, these potential students seemed to accept Tawl's and Zusnis' ideas about interactive delivery strategies and alternative assessment measures, they were obviously unclear as to what was expected of them. They wondered how similar this training would be to the imported training they had become accustomed to modifying. Was this instruction going to be more or less effective with their students?

The SEA trainers indicated that they preferred lecture-based instruction and memory-based assessment measures. Interestingly, it was discovered during the interview process that SEA trainers had been modifying "imported" instruction by *eliminating* the built-in interactive activities and changing the assessment techniques to be more memory, as opposed to performance, based. The SEA trainers indicated that although they "mostly" liked these training programs, they were concerned that their students would be uncomfortable performing in front of their peers and mentioned that losing face was something to be avoided at all costs.

There was an additional concern that students over 40 years of age may not be sufficiently motivated to perform under the nontraditional conditions advocated by the imported programs. These students would be retiring when they turned 55 and mentioned that the time spent learning new skills, at their "mature" age, was "a real waste."

The majority of the trainers interviewed expressed little motivation to attend this new training when it became available. Those who were interviewed mentioned the following concerns:

- Additional time commitments involved in completing a degree program (all worked full time)
- Having to learn a new way of designing and delivering training
- Lack of job advancement, salary compensation, or other rewards or recognition being tied to completion of the program
- Lack of confidence in convincing clients to let them use these new skills

If these concerns were adequately addressed, the trainers indicated that, perhaps, they would participate.

Tawl and Zusnis decided to observe a few training programs currently being offered by the National Training Center. Additional time was spent with the instructors of these courses to determine how their training courses had been developed. In essence, the observations supported what had been suggested in the interviews. SEA trainers were accustomed to presenting and attending instructor-led training. They did not like being put on the spot (performing or responding in front of their peers); they liked assessment measures that provided a quick indication of how much they had learned. Also noted was the fact that they used very little media during instruction and did not engage in either needs analysis or formative evaluation procedures when developing instruction. It was difficult, if not impossible, to determine if any of the training being offered was making a difference on the job.

In contrast to the opinions and preferences mentioned by the SEA trainers, the SEA government strongly supported a move to more "modern" training—it was more than eager to imitate the Americans' approach to the systematic design of instruction. Although Tawl and Zusnis agreed that appropriate teaching methods such as simulations, role plays, and case studies should be used when they supported the instructional objectives of the ID curriculum, they were concerned about motivating the learners to engage in these activities.

Tawl and Zusnis realized that the typical ID competencies needed to be included in a way that fit the needs of the SEA students. Some modifications to a typical ID curriculum would be required. Finally, the question of who should teach the new courses, U.S. or SEA trainers, needed to be addressed. There did not seem to be any easy answers to the many questions facing this experienced design team!

Invoking ID practice via the Frank and Semra case

As Tawl and Zusnis labored to design a blueprint for the ID curriculum, including the identification of the strategies and approaches that should be used, they were faced with a number of difficult decisions. Propose possible solutions for each of the following issues:

▶ How to help the students in this case master factual information and develop intellectual skills and positive attitudes regarding the systems approach to ID

▶ How to motivate learners to use effective learning strategies, including interactive techniques

▶ How to design and evaluate alternative assessment measures (project-based assessments, simulations, role plays, etc.)

▶ How to teach students to use mediated instruction effectively

▶ How to get buy-in for the use of needs assessment and formative evaluation methods

▶ How to build learners' confidence to respond/perform in front of peers

▶ How to motivate the older employees

▶ How to build confidence for working effectively with clients

Case Study 9

Haley Lawrence

by Diane Ehrlich

Over the past seven years, Kadence Communications (KC) has been one of Haley Lawrence's major clients. Her expertise is in health care and she consults as an instructional designer for sales training and management development projects. She recently returned from a national sales meeting in Arizona and was looking forward to a well-deserved break when her phone rang. She listened to a request from Bob Williams, the account executive she usually worked for at Kadence Communications. He explained that KC had been asked to develop sales training for GNA Healthcare, a major player in the highly competitive managed care field. He wanted Lawrence to fly out to a meeting this Friday, September 12.

Lawrence agreed and Williams faxed her a list of GNA people recently brought together by corporate headquarters to spearhead a major training effort.

SEP 09 '97   11:17 AM   Kadence Communications   P. 1

FAX TRANSMITTAL COVER SHEET

To: Haley Lawrence
From: Bob Williams
FAX Number: (555) 788-5483
Date: Tues., September 9, 1997 * 11:17 AM

Transmitting two (2) pages including cover sheet. If there is any difficulty with this transmission, please call (555) 788-5484.

Note:
Haley: Here is the GNA list we talked about. Good luck on Friday!

- **James Sumida,** VP of Human Resources, has been with GNA as a district manager for 10 years, but has only been VP for six months. He has final project approval since training comes out of his budget. Sumida has worked with KC on other projects. This is a high-visibility project—has been given top priority by the president.

- Lynn Katz, currently trains new district managers in the field. She has been with GNA 6 years and taught English prior to that. GNA feels that her teaching experience qualified her as a trainer even though she has no experience in sales.
- Larry Paulsen, has been with the company for 20 years and is considered an expert in managed care.

Not expected at the meeting, but who will be involved in the project, is:

- Carol Califano, a new training specialist who will not start until November. Although she has strong presentation and facilitation skills, she has little knowledge of how to design instruction. She received a President Club Award for District Sales Manager of the Year three years ago.

The meeting was hectic and Lawrence was busy asking questions and taking notes. On the flight home, she reviewed her notes and highlighted the following information:

GNA is committed to training. Brought team into corporate headquarters to spearhead training effort.

Currently 450 sales representatives and 40 district managers. Plan to expand sales force when new product is launched.

Formal two-week training program in place, but 90% of the existing program deals with product knowledge and sales.

Existing training materials include chunks of skills (e.g., one hour on active listening). Doesn't seem to be a coherent, logical design. Lots of paper—little structure. Looks like everyone put in his or her pet ideas. Katz (current trainer) does not seem to have bought into the need for improving training.

Sumida wants to design and develop a three-day sales training workshop for GNA. He wants to use video, audio, and print materials. Doesn't have an extensive budget and isn't quite sure what things cost.

GNA wants the material ASAP, but has allotted about three months for the project to be designed and developed.

Sumida wanted the sales force to have ownership in any new training initiatives and had already assembled a task force made up of regional managers. The task force had been asked to come up with ideas for training needs and had already produced a list of desired content. However, Sumida failed to mention either the task force or the list discussing content during the meeting with Lawrence. Two days later, Lawrence was surprised to receive a fax detailing the content the task force had developed.

INTERPERSONAL SKILLS

External-internal customer relationships; treating customers as business partners; working with different customer personality types; working as part of a sales team; understanding one's own style; looking at sales from a "total office call perspective"; developing new relationships for the future; observation skills; listening skills versus a "how to pounce" attitude; continuity and stages of a sales call; coaching.

SATISFYING CUSTOMER NEEDS

Listening; probing; pre-call planning/post-call analysis; "selling the sizzle"; value-add; benefits orientation.

TARGETING KEY CUSTOMERS

Using data to identify key customers; case studies; 20/80 rule; paradigm shifting for customer base.

STRATEGIC SALES

Service; formularies; selling as a process; tailoring to the customer; positioning products; rewards.

PLANNING

Time management; electronic data support.

Lawrence quickly called Sumida to clarify the project. She had questions about various items on the list, but her primary concern was the amount of information they wanted covered. Sumida assured her that this was a "wish list" for all their training needs, and she breathed a sigh of relief. They wished to develop a *series* of training sessions, but planned to start with the one on building customer relationships. This sounded better to Lawrence. However, the list of material was endless and she realized she needed not only to define terms, but to learn more about the organization. She wasn't sure what a "total office call" was and also had questions about the existing program.

Sumida assured her that she could rely on Califano when she came on board in November, and he suggested that she call Katz in the meantime so they could get started on the project. Katz thought that the training in the field worked well and wasn't sure why Sumida and Califano were redesigning what she did. She mentioned that her training had been well received and resented "outsiders" intervening on her turf. Lawrence reassured Katz that field training would still be an important part of the process, but they were looking to make the training more consistent. She thanked Katz for her help and told her that she would be in touch with her later.

Based on her visit to GNA headquarters and her subsequent telephone conversations with Sumida, Lawrence suggested that the following content should be included in the *Building Customer Relationships* module: quality relationships, personal interaction styles, active listening, and observation. Sumida listened to her suggestions and agreed that the topics sounded good. Lawrence wanted to develop a design document and Sumida thought that was fine, but he also suggested that Lawrence come back to GNA headquarters because they were going to conduct a sales training the following week. Although she thought her time might be more efficiently used, she recognized the advantages of seeing a current sales training session and agreed to attend.

When Lawrence got to GNA, she sat through several hours of training on GNA's major new product initiative. She had a 15-minute meeting with Sumida, and he mentioned that he was reading a book he'd like to see incorporated in the training: Covey's *Seven Habits of Highly Effective People* (1989). She had already noticed that when Sumida addressed the group, he had overheads made from this book and recommended it to the group. He also referred to a book on consultative selling. Lawrence noticed that only about half of the audience knew this book; the other half of the group looked confused.

Lawrence questioned him later about the book and he mentioned that part of the original group had gone through training on this consultative sales model. When she asked for the title of the book, Sumida provided it. However, he didn't think she needed to read it—he thought she should just start designing the program because time was short. She also noticed several effective role plays that were part of the training, and Sumida mentioned that GNA videotaped and reviewed these "clinics" during each of their training sessions. He requested that similar videotaped role plays be included in the proposed training. Lawrence thought that was an excellent idea from an instructional point of view but expressed concern about cost.

On the flight home, she listed several concerns she had with the project. She decided to discuss these with Sumida during their next telephone call, but after two days, he still had not called. He had left on a two-week vacation. Califano mentioned that he was out of town and that she was in charge. Lawrence asked if she could send a design document to her for review (Figure 9.1). Califano thought the design document looked fine and told Lawrence to go ahead with the units.

Three days later Lawrence sent a copy of the unit on active listening to Califano for review. Although it was only 15 pages, Lawrence wanted to see if the format would work for the other units in this module on interpersonal skills. Califano agreed to review the materials but told Lawrence that she might not get to it until the following week.

With less than five weeks before the training was to be presented, time was increasingly becoming an issue. Lawrence continued writing the unit on observation skills without either Califano's or Sumida's feedback on the previous unit. She then sent the second unit to both and waited a few days before calling. Sumida thought it was great. Califano sent a few pages with grammatical changes but said she liked the

Figure 9.1   Module 1: Building Customer Relationships

Objective	Materials	Time
Participants will define what a quality relationship is from their own perspective.	Worksheet Flip chart	20 minutes
Participants will learn how others define a quality relationship.	Print and video	1 hour
Participants will identify their personal styles.	Personality profile Worksheets Discussion	1.5–1.75 hours, including debriefing
Participants will demonstrate active listening skills.	Role play	1 hour, including debriefing
Participants will demonstrate their ability to be perceptive observers.	Observation model exercise	45 minutes

format. Sumida sent copies to Katz, Paulsen, and three other people to review. Each had suggested changes—some minor, some major. Katz had major concerns about the whole approach to teaching observation skills. She also questioned the decision to have role play as the primary method of teaching listening skills. Paulsen didn't like many of the self-assessment questions in the unit on observation skills. Tim Anderson, who had been part of the task force of district managers, liked the questions but thought that they should be formatted differently.

Lawrence became increasingly frustrated and decided it was time to set up another meeting with the team. This time Paulsen, Califano, Katz, and Sumida were all there. Lawrence presented an overview of the project and mentioned that they only had four weeks before the first sales school. She suggested that they do a "run-through" in two weeks so that any changes could be made. At this point Sumida brought up the idea of the video again and asked who in Lawerence's group could produce a video. Lawrence mentioned that production costs would be at least twice what it would cost to produce in-house and suggested that they use their own video department. She suggested using their own people as experts on how to sell instead of actors to further reduce costs.

Lawrence and Sumida disagreed as to the number of sales representatives to be interviewed and who they would be. He asked who she was planning to interview and she suggested a cross-section of reps in rural and urban territories, as well as both newer and experienced reps so that they all would have "buy-in" to the quality relationship idea. Sumida and Califano eventually agreed on five people and then found a sixth. Lawrence and Sumida also disagreed on how the tape should be used during the training. Lawrence suggested that they table that discussion until after they saw the tape. Sumida agreed.

A week later, he called Lawrence and suggested she come to their home office and see the tape. Given the limited budget available for the project, she was surprised at the suggestion of another trip to view the videotape. She suggested that they send a copy of the tape to her and pointed out that they would save money on her plane fare and her time could be better spent finishing up the last two modules. Sumida assented.

When Lawrence viewed the tape, she suggested condensing it. Sumida proposed that the group meet. She suggested a conference call. The videotape was not part of their original contract, and she was concerned about the amount of time and attention this was taking from the original project agreement. After a phone discussion, the group finally eliminated one of the interviews and edited one of the interviews and some of the interview questions. Sumida seemed content with the video.

There was only one week left before the project deadline and Lawrence had yet to receive comments on the final two units. She spoke to both Sumida and Califano, and neither seemed to see the urgency. They weren't too concerned until she discussed the consequences of making last-minute changes. They decided to have the material copied by their copy center and sent out. Lawrence was relieved not to have to worry about making copies and shipping them.

The night before the project, Sumida was still making changes. Lawrence was upset but had been in the consulting business long enough to know that was par for the course. She suggested that instead of running off the 500 copies he had wanted, they only print enough copies for the pilot sales class in case they needed to make changes. She would spend the three days at GNA with a colleague evaluating the program and discussing its effectiveness with participants. Although reluctant at first, Sumida agreed.

Some of the trainers didn't follow the schedule because they didn't seem to know how to limit the discussion. Lawrence made careful notes on how to target the discussions so that the program could be adapted and still fit within the allotted time. The pilot test provided a lot of information, and the team decided to meet and make one last set of revisions before duplicating an entire set of materials. At that meeting, Sumida looked at Lawrence and suggested that they start on the second module. She said she was interested in continuing to work with the group but that she had several concerns.

Invoking ID practice via the Haley Lawrence case

1. What are the major problems in this situation from Lawrence's point of view? How could Lawrence have avoided these problems?

2. Discuss Lawrence's performance as a consultant. If you were at the first meeting with the client, what advice would you have given her as to how to proceed?

3. Discuss Lawrence's performance as a designer. Using any ID model of your choice, describe how she addressed the various elements of the design process.

4. What suggestions do you have for Lawrence now that the client wishes to move on to the next stage of the project?

REFERENCES

Covey, S. R. (1989). *The seven habits of highly effective people.* New York: Simon & Schuster.

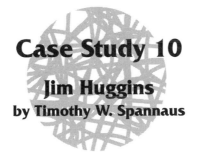

Case Study 10

Jim Huggins

by Timothy W. Spannaus

Jim Huggins sat and stared at the report just delivered to him on the use of a large-scale computer-based training (CBT) innovation on which he had worked for most of the last two years. His client, Hill Industries, a leading, high-tech manufacturing organization, had spent several million dollars developing a large-scale CBT system for training employees on a new product development (PD) process. He could not believe the information he was reading. Repeatedly, he read through the executive summary:

> Relatively few members of the target population were actually using the CBT, probably less than 15%. The total target population was over 15,000, and based on survey data, less than 3000 used the CBT on a regular basis.

> Engineers in the target population were more inclined to ask a local expert for technical information than to consult the CBT, even though the CBT information was generally more current and more accurate than the local expert.

> Process development leaders reported that in their meetings with program teams, people didn't have information that was available from the CBT.

> Process development leaders relied heavily on the CBT to distribute current information about the PD process. They were disappointed to find that their information was not getting out to the whole company as they thought it was. They had become so dependent on the CBT that they no longer used any other mass communication tool.

> Many members of the target population did not get an opportunity to practice using the CBT to solve process design problems.

"...probably less than 15% ... used the CBT on a regular basis"—over and over again, Huggins stared at this finding. Any one of the findings by itself was extremely unfavorable, but together they constituted a major failure of the project. What, if anything, could be done to salvage the project at this stage? As the reality of the survey results began to settle in his mind, Huggins looked back over the course of the project searching for clues as to why the CBT innovation might have so clearly failed to achieve its objectives ....

Hill Industries was a large, high-tech producer of manufacturing plant machinery. The machinery was complex, with a lot of variety in what customers wanted as accessories or configuration (power, custom tooling, capacity). Although basically mechanical, the machinery had an increasingly electronic dimension (controls, communications, instruments). In earlier decades, when the range of products wasn't as great, the products were not as complicated, and there were fewer government regulations, the company could design and produce a totally new product in about two years, with a small team. However, over the years, the process and the product became more complex and more expensive. Everyone in the domestic and European segments of the industry was experiencing the same problem of increasing costs and longer product cycles.

In addition, in the last ten years, new companies, both domestic and foreign, entered the business. Their agility and speed took market share from the old-line companies. The new companies seemed to have new products every year or so. The products were very good and less expensive. These new products were selling well and indeed, some old-line manufacturers went out of business, merged, or were in bankruptcy. At the same time, the market seemed to demand a greater variety of machines. The new competitors, with their fast time to market, could launch new products much faster than the older companies could.

Hill Industries responded to the competitive threat by revamping the PD process, trying to reduce time and cost while improving quality. Typically, this process took years to complete, from the initial idea to delivering a new product to the first customer. An idea for a new product might have involved improvements to an existing product (known as a *freshening* or *mid-life kicker*) or a totally new line of products, perhaps a line of small presses for use by job shops. If it was a freshening, the PD process could require a couple of years. A totally new product might have required six or seven years, especially if a new manufacturing plant was required.

The PD process was the responsibility of the product development organization (PDO). Under the old process, PDO had coordinated work by various functional organizations in Hill, such as design, engineering, marketing, and so on. Now PDO was to form teams for each new product and assign a project manager, who was in charge of schedule, budget, quality, staffing, facilities, and all the things that are the responsibility of any project manager. There were milestones to be met, defined by deliverables, quality criteria, dates, and responsibilities. Such milestones included Concept Approval, Tooling, Prototype Approvals, Pilot Assembly, Mass Production, and so on. Teams consisted of people from engineering, testing, design, manufacturing, marketing, finance, purchasing, and all the affected functions of the company. There were also suppliers on the team, since the company purchased about 40 percent of the content of the product, including most of the electronics, plastic parts, cabinets, and so on. Most people in PDO went from team to team, spending from two to seven years on a team.

The new PD process at Hill Industries had a flatter organization (fewer middle managers), fewer approval steps by executive management, fewer prototypes, early involvement of manufacturing and marketing, more reliance on design and engineering, and a wide variety of other changes. The process included over 10,000 people at major company locations in North America and Europe, and smaller groups with affiliated companies in Pacific Rim countries and South America.

Such major changes in the PD process created a need for a variety of training interventions, and a steering committee was convened to take on responsibility for PD training. The steering committee included representatives of the process owners (high-level executives with responsibility for defining and maintaining the PD process); members of the training department; and representatives of senior management, who were under pressure to accelerate the PD process while cutting costs. The chair of the committee was Bob Werner, a recent retiree who had returned to take charge of implementing the new PD process. He had gained a lot of respect in his years as the program director of some very successful product launches. The committee also hired Huggins as an instructional design (ID) consultant because of his long experience in designing technical training and using technology to deliver training.

The steering committee quickly decided that time was a critical factor: whatever training was needed had to be done quickly. Competitive pressure, particularly from foreign manufacturers, required improved quality, faster product development, and reduced costs. The steering committee concluded that the time factor alone ruled out classroom training since the organization could not deliver it to everyone who needed training (15,000 salaried people) in a reasonable time frame. This decision was confirmed by the fact that the PD process continued to change quickly enough that Hill Industries could not get its personnel through before it changed again.

The first training initiative was a one-day "Overview" class. So much of the new PD process depended on cross-functional teams that the steering committee asked for a class to address that issue specifically. Product development teams were new to Hill, so people did not really know how they would work.

Huggins' company responded with a highly interactive class based on case studies. For each case study, the class broke into small teams, with each team including people from design, engineering, manufacturing, and finance. Each team then worked through real PD problems, using the new PD process. The class design emphasized working together in cross-disciplinary teams. The faculty team for each class session included an experienced PD engineer and a team facilitator, to make sure both the PD process and the team function objectives were met. The "Overview" class was immediately implemented throughout the organization as part of the PD training process.

In the meantime, Huggins had been given primary responsibility for determining training delivery methods for the remainder of the content and was asked to present a report detailing preferred delivery methods to the steering committee. After several weeks of analysis of current and projected resources, he presented his report to a regular meeting of the steering committee:

"I suggest that our response to the PD process training problem is to design and develop a hypermedia computer-based training program. Since every member of the target population has a PC on the desktop, most of which are soon to be on networks connected by a backbone wide-area network (WAN), we already have the technical infrastructure to implement such a program.

"The CBT will provide information on the PD process including design, engineering, testing, finance, product management, and product planning. The hypermedia will provide text and graphics with extensive links among processes, organizations, and product subsystems. The typical screen for the hypertext CBT will include text and graphics. Terms in the text will be linked to glossary definitions of the term. The graphic area will include links to additional details, usually provided as pop-up boxes on the current page. So users will have ready access to a lot of information, with ready access to additional levels of detail if they choose to use it. Additional changes to the PD process could be quickly included in the CBT and distributed over the network.

"The user will also be able to follow links between processes, so for example, when he or she is learning the prototyping process, relevant financial or manufacturing information will be available by taking links from the prototyping pages. Those links might detail the financial requirements for prototype approval or manufacturing's involvement in prototyping."

The committee listened politely to the recommendation, then sat silently. They then started asking questions indicating they didn't understand what this recommendation had to do with training. "Do people go to the classes first and then use this CBT? I don't understand how it works," said one committee member. "Do you have a class for each process, like we had before?" asked another.

Huggins had thought the case for CBT was so obvious he wasn't expecting much opposition. He took a deep breath and explained there were no classes, other than the "Overview" that had been running for several weeks now. He referred them back to the audience and context analyses he had conducted to show that the size of the audience, its diversity, and the amount of time required for training all meant that sit-down classes would not work well. He reminded them of all their complaints about the previous classes, how long they'd taken, how they never seemed to be available when people needed them, how much money the instructors cost, and what it cost to update the class materials.

Some committee members nodded in agreement, but not many. John Eggleston, a training supervisor in PDO, understood exactly what Huggins was saying. Over the years Eggleston had worked in this very traditional training environment ("butts in seats") and had noted widespread unhappiness with previous PD training. But knowing what was wrong with classroom training was a long way from jumping to CBT. "Can people actually learn from CBT? I mean, we've had some here and it was pretty bad. People just had to read text from the screen. No one liked it. I don't think that's what we want to do here. I've seen some CBT for computer skills, but that's not what this is about. Has anyone used CBT for this kind of training?"

In an attempt to respond to some of these questions and objections, Huggins offered to put together a paper describing some history of CBT, how various companies used it, and how it could be done effectively. The committee readily accepted the offer and agreed to meet one week later. In a week, Huggins brought his paper in and presented it to the committee. He cited academic studies showing that people learn from CBT and that CBT takes less time. Then he summarized case studies from other large companies demonstrating that what he was proposing was not new or leading edge, but fairly common practice. He also cited other groups in Hill Industries that had some experience with CBT, to defuse the concern that PDO was breaking new ground.

The committee liked what they read but still needed more. The idea of adopting CBT for such important training made them nervous. They didn't really know how it would work or how people in PDO would react to it. Werner, the steering committee chair, suggested they benchmark the companies Huggins cited, plus any others they could find that used CBT for engineering training. While he had little training experience and almost no experience with computers (which he often called "confusers"), his daughter worked for a software company. In the week between meetings, he had called her to ask her if CBT made any sense. She listed some potential problems, but basically gave her approval to the idea. With her approval and Huggins' paper, Wermer was ready to press the case for CBT. As a program director he had always pushed for inclusion of new technology. CBT seemed like just another technology they should adopt. Werner led the benchmarking effort, gaining confidence with each conference call to training managers, project managers, and engineers in several other companies.

With Werner on board, Huggins felt more confident the proposal would work, but they still had many committee members to convince.

Several of the companies mentioned a concern associated with the cost of developing CBT. Several members of the steering committee, including Eggleston, seized on that issue, calling it a show-stopper. Werner arranged for Huggins to meet with a manager in finance, who helped put together a cost-benefit analysis for the project. Huggins knew the importance of using trusted numbers and stating any assumptions so the analysis would be solid. However, he also knew that, while he often had to do cost-benefit analyses to get CBT projects going, they never really convinced anyone to go ahead. In any event, the cost-benefit was better than expected. The project would pay for itself within six months, before all the CBT was even developed.

Huggins and Werner reviewed their progress. They had shown that CBT would work by getting case studies from other companies. They had shown that it would pay for itself, though there was a high front-end cost for design and development. But there were still important and vocal members of the committee who weren't on board.

Werner decided to push the committee really hard at the next meeting to try to get their approval to go ahead. As an engineer and successful manager, he was used to making decisions even when full information was not available, confident that they would be able to make the CBT work. He felt frustrated that the training community didn't seem to work the same way. At the next meeting, Werner laid out the case while Huggins listened to the objections. Finally, he realized that the problem was that the committee members could not visualize the CBT. Their idea of CBT was based on some pretty awful mainframe CBT they had seen years ago. Huggins offered to build a prototype they could try out with their own engineers—they could use their new process as the content. If it worked, the cost would be reasonable and the risk for both the company and the consultant would be low.

While Huggins huddled with a senior instructional designer and operations manager to figure out what to prototype and how much to charge, Werner presented the proposal to the committee. Quick agreement came when the price for the prototype was less than the committee had agreed they would be willing to spend. Werner was pretty sure most of the committee didn't know what they had just bought, but agreeing to the prototype served the purpose of moving the decision process along.

Within Huggins' company the work now shifted from a consulting and change effort to CBT design and development. Working with subject-matter experts from the committee, he led the effort to put together a demo module for the committee to review. The attractive, easy-to-use program worked. The committee now understood what it was Huggins and Werner were trying to do but questioned the start-up of the CBT. Huggins proposed that as employees complete the "Overview" class, they be given access to the CBT. The committee agreed to this and to go ahead with development of the CBT.

Huggins worked with Leslie Santulli, the operations manager, to put together his design and development team, including subject-matter experts from the steering committee. The team prioritized modules, built schedules, allocated resources, and established review schedules. Development was finally underway.

In the meantime, Eggleston and Werner worked on implementation issues. Hill Industries, rather than Huggins' consulting firm, had taken responsibility for implementation. Their approach was to use the training coordinators already in place throughout the company to lead the way. Their implementation plan consisted of meetings of the training coordinators in which they demonstrated the new CBT and directed them to ensure that employees have access to the CBT from their desktop computers.

This top-down approach was not very participative but was consistent with the corporate culture. Many of the coordinators saw their value to the company as advising employees, monitoring training plans, and scheduling classes efficiently for their organization. They did a terrific job of making sure people registered for and completed the PD "Overview" class.

One year later, many thousands of engineers, analysts, managers, and planners had completed this class. Yet only a few thousand had used the CBT at all, even though by now there were 10 modules, about 15 hours of instruction.

To try to get a handle on why implementation was so slow, the steering committee commissioned a formal study by a third-party evaluator. The evaluator's first task was to determine how much the CBT was being used. A month later she was back with her report. Huggins sat down to read his copy.

Invoking ID practice via the Jim Huggins case

1. Evaluate Jim Huggins' performance in convincing the steering committee to adopt CBT.
2. What obstacles in Hill Industries may have caused such a low level of adoption of CBT?
3. What factors supported the adoption of CBT within Hill Industries?
4. What could be done at this stage to increase usage of CBT within the organization?

Case Study 11

Julie Tatano: Harvesting Cooperation
by Ann Kovalchick, Mable B. Kinzie, Marti F. Julian, and M. Elizabeth Hrabe

Date: Mon, 17 March, 1997 15:54:35
X-Sender: swashing@bigben.franklinstate.edu
Mime-Version: 1.0
To: tatano@bigben.franklinstate.edu
From: stew@franklinstate.edu (Stewart Washington)
Subject: project meeting
Status: RO

Julie,

The meeting went well don't you think? A lot of good
ideas were presented. I liked Sam's thoughts about the
workshops. We need to get some product out there and
this might be the right opportunity. Billie wants the
Ag College to establish a high profile, and she's
determined to get outside funding for this project, I
bet a CD-ROM will get some attention. We could produce
a CD-ROM and include all 20 years worth of Joe's radio
programs! It's a great storage technology for interactive development (we'll need to add pictures). Would
you send Darlene a note and ask her to set up the mail
list you suggested? I'm meeting with the Provost this
afternoon (she'll LOVE this project), Let's talk when I
get back. Brush up on your Java script! Toolbook?
Authorware? Director? What do you think?
Stewart
****

Stewart Washington, Director
Technology and Learning Resource Center
Franklin State University
(993) 798-8973

Men hoist the banner of the ideal, and then march in
the direction that concrete conditions suggest and reward.

-- John Dewey, "The Quest for Certainty"

Washington's e-mail expressed the same unconstrained excitement for technology that Tatano had detected in the recent *Keystone Alumni* article describing the opening of Franklin State University's Technology and Learning Resource Center (TLRC). She was pleased that her award-winning design project "Art in My World" had been cited as providing the foundation for the TLRC's future success, but warning lights went off in her head when she read that Washington defined that success as "building a reputation as a leader in innovative courseware on CD-ROM." After all, the effectiveness of "Art in My World" had more to do with the way the curriculum empowered students to speak out about their community than with the minimal role technology played as a delivery and presentation medium. After meeting with Washington and the faculty from the Agriculture College and extension office, Tatano worried that the unfocused goals of this current project might create a vacuum into which Washington would inject his "technology solutions." Although the project dynamics would be dicey—there were a lot of strong personalities involved—Tatano *had* worked well with the faculty of the art department and felt confident that she could effectively steer the project content experts through a thorough needs assessment.

Among the folks involved with the project, tentatively titled "This Land is Your Land," Jorge Recinos was the only one not at the initial planning meeting. Recinos was the director of the Franklin Area Youth Action Project (FAYAP) and a key stakeholder. Tatano was glad she had called him immediately after the meeting, though Billie Redmond provided his phone number only as an afterthought. Recinos was an active and outspoken leader and advocate for the growing migrant community in Franklin County. Aware of the increasing anti-immigrant sentiment taking hold across the region, he was concerned about high school–aged migrant youth, especially those from families "settling out," or choosing to put down roots in the community. Redmond was an adjunct associate professor at the Agriculture College and an outreach specialist for the Boone Valley Extension office; she had her hands full developing community workshops for the extension office. She was anxious to use the World Wide Web in her fall course, "Special Topics in Farm Management." When she learned that Recinos wanted to develop a distance education project she recognized it as a golden opportunity and had asked Stewart how the TRLC could assist. However, after Tatano spoke with Recinos, she had a far different take on the learner population than she had from the initial planning meeting, where the focus had been on Redmond's course needs.

Many of the youth that Recinos worked with had spent 10 years or more in the community, attended public schools, and were serious students. In many ways they were bicultural, with good English language skills and the same basic dreams as their rural American counterparts (e.g., a pickup truck in the driveway of a ranch house with enough acreage to support some livestock and crops). Unfortunately, Recinos had seen too many high school youth end up back in the field *piscando,* or picking, even though many of them wished to own their own farms one day. After securing $6000 in donations from local businesses to purchase computers for his community center, Recinos decided to use the university's resources to provide Hispanic youth interested in farming careers with access to materials and mentors from the Ag College and the extension office.

▶ Tuesday, 25 March

Tatano had been looking forward to this afternoon's project meeting. Over the past week she reviewed the perspectives of each project stakeholder and felt armed with a more complete understanding of each individual's interest than at the initial meeting. She hoped to convey the purpose of conducting a thorough needs assessment by explaining how this would highlight learner needs and appropriate instructional strategies and media selection. Her greatest concerns were the expectations of Sam Kellerman, Extension Services Coordinator, and Joe Dagsworthy, a senior faculty member of Franklin State University's College of Agriculture. Both men had been active members of the local farm community for nearly 35 years. Kellerman liked the idea of developing an outreach project aimed at youth and had told Tatano that "vocational training was something we need to do more of." Like Kellerman, Dagsworthy considered himself an expert on outreach efforts and had spent much of their conversation describing the history and process of the diffusion of innovations in agriculture. When he unexpectedly suggested that Tatano simply re-script his weekly Sunday afternoon radio programs on farm issues to re-purpose them into instructional videos, Tatano was afraid that her silence may have been interpreted as agreement. Neither Kellerman nor Dagsworthy seemed much in tune with the needs of a Hispanic youth population.

From Washington's perspective, the only needs that Tatano should be concerned with were those of the Ag College faculty. He told her, "They know how to teach their content, give 'em what they want!" While her work relationship with him was good, Tatano often felt that Washington was too apt to take the path of least resistance and far more interested in what she considered gimmicks, such as the "just-in-time" learning model that he thought fit this project. She knew that he always supported his staff, yet with his background in computer science and as the former director of Academic Computing Services, Tatano thought that Washington knew little about the formal design of instruction and principles of learning. Now he worked closely with the provost with the goal of infusing technology into the university. At the moment, he saw the Ag school project as an opportunity to apply for a $10,000 grant funded by the Provost's office for developing multimedia courseware.

It wasn't until her brief chat with Redmond just before that day's project meeting that Tatano realized how resistant Dagsworthy was to working with the TRLC, preferring instead to work with the KFSB-AM production staff who produced his radio programs. However, Redmond considered him an important player, given his community prominence.

Tatano was disappointed when neither Kellerman nor Dagsworthy showed up at the meeting since she had hoped to try to invest them more thoroughly into the project. Redmond had remarked that "Joe's not even interested in writing his radio scripts using a word processor...he's happy with his IBM electric!" Now Tatano suspected that Dagsworthy, and possibly Kellerman, didn't even use e-mail and likely hadn't received her postings announcing the meeting time and place. She'd have to contact them in person to let them know that Redmond and Recinos had agreed that a course covering Integrated Pest Management (IPM) would be useful. Recinos thought that it would help his kids get ahead of the curve on farm management and, since he assumed that they would learn to use the Internet, he could give them an incentive by offering them a certificate in Technology and Farm Management. Tatano worried that this was a far cry from what Kellerman and Dagsworthy were expecting. At least Redmond, Recinos, and Washington had all agreed that this first project should be conceived as a pilot project.

Friday 28 March

The meeting with Kellerman and Dagsworthy had not gone well. Kellerman kept referring to the learning population as "Spanish kids" and, like Dagsworthy, expected the materials to address all high school age youth rather than focus on Hispanic youth. Dagsworthy even suggested that "kids aren't that different when you come right down to it." In addition, he restated that he considered his weekly half-hour radio programs a valuable community service and saw no reason they couldn't be used. He was particularly unenthusiastic about the topic of IPM, something he considered a "way-out idea." At least it made more sense to Kellerman when he considered that IPM would also be the focus of Redmond's "Special Topics" course planned for the fall. The meeting ended abruptly with Kellerman telling Tatano to "see what she could do." Tomorrow she would be conducting a focus group with several of the kids that Recinos said were interested in the course he wanted to offer. By now Tatano felt she was juggling too many divergent perspectives and expectations for the same project. She wondered if conducting a focus group and learning of even more perspectives was a good idea?

▶ Thursday 3 April

Tatano returned to her office after the morning's project meeting and wondered if it was wise to interpret Kellerman and Dagsworthy's easy agreement to her presentation of the project's needs and goals as a go-ahead. Had she managed to please everyone? As she penciled in the next project meeting scheduled for two weeks hence (she would present a design proposal then), she wondered if the worst was over. Taking a quick glance at the handout of the Table of Needs that she had discussed

Figure 11.1   Table of Needs and Summary Points

Table of Needs
Overall Project Goals

Desired Performance	Current Performance
1. To provide nonformal, community-based instruction in agriculture education and farm management that provides opportunities for student-teacher interaction and that can be accessed using online, electronic technology.	1. Students are busy and spend a large part of their time in traditional instructional environments.
2. To provide opportunities for Hispanic youth to develop networking and community partnership skills among peers and leaders in the farm community.	2. Cultural differences have resulted in isolation and stereotyping.

Pilot Program Needs

Desired Performance	Current Performance
Hispanic high school students in the FAYAP program:	
1. Will be able to access Integrated Pest Management (IPM) information via the Internet.	1. Minimal experience with Internet-based technologies.
2. Will be able to define IPM using appropriate technical terms and concepts.	2. Minimal and nonformal knowledge of concepts and technical language commonly used for pest management strategies.

(continued on next page)

Figure 11.1 *Continued*

Desired Performance	Current Performance
3. Will be able to explain IPM strategies to potential users.	3. Limited opportunities to practice professional communication skills.

Needs Analysis Summary Points

Institutional

Source	Conclusion
Project proposal provided by Jorge Recinos	Few established ties between FSU and the Hispanic youth population make the university a potentially uncomfortable and unfamiliar learning environment.
Boone Valley Cooperative Extension	Library of archived outreach efforts indicates previous community-based education, with focus on radio and video programs.
TRLC	New technology production facility and two technical support staff (15–25% time) for innovative technology-based projects is available, as well as 50 MB of UNIX server space available for project files.
College of Agriculture	This is their first attempt at outreach based on computer-based technologies. Currently there is limited use of digital technologies for instruction.

Social

Source	Conclusion
Joe Dagsworthy	Joe Dagsworthy would like to incorporate 23 years of radio programs on farming and can provide some content resources.
Joe Dagsworthy and Sam Kellerman	Both consider outreach efforts to function via a diffusion process and seek a possible wider audience. Sam Kellerman is

(continued on next page)

Figure 11.1 *Continued*

Source	Conclusion
	especially interested in vocational training and the use of work shops. Joe Dagsworthy is interested in use of videotape.
Billie Redmond	Billie Redmond teaches a course on Special Topics in Farm Management. Her personal academic interest is in using World Wide Web technologies for innovative instruction for her Fall course on "Integrated Pest Management."
Project Proposal (Jorge Recinos)	1. Limited opportunity for economic advancement due to stereotypical perceptions regarding farm worker families. 2. Learning population at-risk in terms of education and professional opportunity beyond high school. 3. Learning population's minority cultural status makes networking within wider community difficult.
Focus Group Discussion	1. Hispanic youth are familiar with the basic responsibilities of farm management and consider it a viable occupation. 2. Important skills and knowledge for successful farm managers: Primary a. Technical language competency. b. People skills needed for employee supervision and professional networking. c. Decision-making and planning skills. Secondary a. Working under pressure. b. Assessing risks. c. Knowledge of pesticides and insecticides, including federal regulations.

(continued on next page)

Figure 11.1 *Continued*

Source	Conclusion
	d. Knowledge of packaging and shipping.
	e. Financial management.
	f. Record keeping.
	3. Currently they do not consider the high school curriculum relevant to their needs or interests. They've expressed concern over the pace at which subject areas were covered in school.
Observations of target population	1. Basic language skills sufficient.
	2. Male and female learners.
Jorge Recinos	1. Learning population age approximately 16–18 and in junior and senior year of high school.
	2. Plans to offer a certificate of completion in Technology and Farm Management.
Second Project Planning Meeting	1. Total number of potential project participants may vary between 20 and 30. Initial enrollment will be limited to 10.
	2. Focus initial effort on IPM strategies.

Physical

Source	Conclusion
Focus-group discussion	1. Erratic scheduling due to part-time jobs.
	2. Occasional transportation problems.
Jorge Recinos	Networked computers available at FAYAP community center, open and staffed with part-time staff M–F 10:00 A.M.–10:00 P.M. and Saturday 11:00 A.M.–7:00 P.M.

in the meeting, as well as her own notes on the needs analysis summary points, she had the vague sense that the needs assessment phase was not complete (Figure 11.1). Still, there wasn't much time. She had to move on...

Invoking ID practice via the Julie Tatano case

1. Describe how designers can advocate for and demonstrate their critical role in given projects.
2. Indicate information needed from a thorough needs assessment. Recommend/create appropriate instruments for gathering the needed information.
3. Critique the goals that Tatano presented in her Table of Needs.
4. Discuss factors to consider during the media selection process.
5. Recommend strategies for dealing with multiple perspectives regarding project purpose and function.

Case Study 12

Karen Cole

by Katherine S. Cennamo

Karen Cole wondered if this would be her big break! Here she was, in her second year of a master's program in instructional technology, with no job prospects in sight, and all of a sudden, a big project fell into her lap...

▶ Mid-September, Cole's Journal Entry

Although I'm graduating soon, I really want to stay in the Central State University area. My husband has a good job. I always hoped I would be able to find work close to the university. If not, I don't know if Steve will be willing to move. Should I go back to my old job teaching preschool? Maybe I won't have to worry about these things much longer. I've got a great chance to prove my skills with this big project. And it's on campus too! I know it's just a demonstration project for the Interactive Technology Center, but CSU has just received funding to hire a full-time director for the center. Maybe it will be me!

Right now, the center is a "self-serve" lab full of high-powered computers. In fact, I'm very familiar with the machines and software housed there. I've served as a lab assistant in the center for my entire master's program. I'm supposed to help faculty use the computers and software for course development, but realistically, the center is rarely used. Sometimes a faculty member stops by to develop a conference presentation, but the interactive multimedia capabilities in the center are basically untouched by the faculty. For the most part, the capabilities of the computer systems are explored only by the lab staff on duty. After all, it gets pretty boring just sitting around waiting for faculty to show up. In fact, it was during one of these exploratory sessions that I got this project. Vice President Lucas was touring the facility with some guests while I was playing around with the equipment. The next thing I knew, V-P Lucas had hired *me* to develop an interactive program for the campus Admissions office.

Mid-September, From the Desk of Vice President Lucas

Boy, I hope Karen gets on this project soon. When I took Mr. and Mrs. Bowman through the Interactive Multimedia Center, I was really glad that Karen was there. These folks are the major funders of the center. And it was a little embarrassing that the room full of expensive equipment was not being used except by Karen. After all, the Bowmans donated the money for all of those computers! The things Karen was doing must have impressed them! They were quite jolly as we were leaving the center. But when they asked when they'd be able to see some products that had been developed there, I thought I'd better work quick. And that's when I came up with the idea for Admissions.

Mid-September, Cole's Journal Entry

Admissions wants to take the new program on the road for recruiting purposes. It's supposed to showcase each program area in the entire college. Although it's mid-September already, they want it by the end of December so they can use it for their major recruiting drive. No problem! This is my big chance to show my stuff! And if it is successful...

Early October, Cole's Journal Entry

Today is the day! Vice President Lucas put together an advisory committee of faculty and high-level administrators to work with me on this project. I've been charged with creating an interactive program that showcases the programs of the college. Everyone wants it to be sensational! In fact, the Development Office is talking about using the program to show to potential donors. And the Visitors' Center has already requested a copy. Today I meet with my advisory group for the first time. Dr. Lucas asked me to make a short presentation to the group about multimedia. But I'm not worried! I already have a presentation available—one that I gave in my computer class last semester. It worked well then (I got an "A") so there's no reason to believe it won't work for this group. After all, it's already been tried out!

Later in October, From the Desk of Vice President Lucas

After the meeting, several advisory committee members commented on the "low level" of Karen's presentation. I wonder what they meant by that? It seemed fine to me. I hope they get over these feelings soon! I don't have time to attend these meetings myself. After all, Karen is in charge of developing this thing.

November, Cole's Journal Entry

What am I going to do with this project? We meet once a week, and I always take notes about what they want. I keep working right along, but the committee is always changing its mind. They seem so concerned about minute details! I try to please them but one week when we meet, they want this; the next week they want that! Several of them have started stopping by the center to see how it's going. As soon as I make the changes one person suggests, someone wants another one! It's hard to please 12 different people. I wish V-P Lucas would show up for some of these meetings. I need to tell him that I may not make the December deadline!

Late January, Vice President Lucas's Journal Entry

Boy, the Admissions people are really upset! Karen doesn't have that multimedia program ready for them to show to high school students during their recruiting drive. I'd forgotten about it, to be honest. I got so busy with other things, and since I hadn't heard from Karen, I thought things were moving along just fine. After all, she has a team of faculty and administrators advising her. Oh, I heard old Joe grumbling about what a sloppy job she was doing, but it's awfully hard to please Joe! I know! I've known him for a long time. I'll have to get over to see Karen sometime. We just have to have something to show Mr. and Mrs. Bowman next time they are on campus.

Early May, Cole's Journal Entry

Well, I've finally got something that works! I worked all day and night, for weeks it seems, but I've got a product to show off for Parents' Day. And maybe it doesn't have *everything* that everyone wants in it, but it looks pretty good! And it's already installed in *four kiosks* in the Visitors' Center, ready for Parents' Day.

Later in May, From the Desk of Vice President Lucas

Wow! Do I have a mess on my hands! It was Parents' Day. People were all over campus. And lots of folks stopped by our interactive kiosks in the Visitors' Center. But what a nightmare. The programs were crashing left and right! Of course by the time Mr. and Mrs. Bowman showed up with their friends, all four of the demonstrations were already down! What _went wrong? It worked fine when Karen demonstrated it for me. What do we do now? How can we save face?_

You have been hired as a consultant by Dr. Lucas. You are to identify what went wrong and outline a plan to save face. Consider the following issues:

Invoking ID practice via the Karen Cole case

1. Identify initial problems with the project in terms of the ID process.
2. Describe strategies for managing ID projects effectively.
3. Suggest ways that an ID project manager might successfully interact with an advisory committee.
4. Describe how Cole could have evaluated the project during various stages of development.
5. Discuss ways to salvage a project that has severe problems such as the ones Cole faces at the end of this case.

Case Study 13

Kathryn O'Neill
by Molly H. Baker

Kathryn O'Neill had looked forward to working with college faculty ever since she had left her own teaching job to complete a degree in instructional design (ID). Her enthusiasm for using technology, trying new approaches to teaching, and working collaboratively with colleagues had led her to shift her career from teaching content to providing faculty support for integrating technology into higher education. One of her principal tasks, the dean had emphasized during her job interview last month, would be to ensure success in the college's new venture into distance education. He stressed the importance of reaching out to underserved regions of the state as a means of boosting student credit hours while establishing degree programs before some of the "competition." Since O'Neill had completed her internship and dissertation in distance learning, she was looking forward to the opportunity to share her enthusiasm, insights, and newly practiced consulting skills. Soon after her arrival, she was given a list of faculty who would be teaching on the new interactive television system. One of the names was Dr. Joseph Johnson from the Elementary Education Department.

Dr. Johnson was a full professor with 14 years of college teaching experience. He had won several teaching awards and liked knowing that he had a reputation for being a risk taker and an independent thinker. Over the past few years, he had taught a methods course in a variety of formats (weekly, weekend academy, independent study, and so on), and had recently been asked to be the first one in his department to teach the course on the interactive television system. Reaching a new group of students in a part of the state underserved by any university appealed to him as well, because his department had been experiencing some decline in enrollment this year. Since he had not been using technology much in his traditional classes, he was a little concerned about dealing with the equipment, but had been assured by his department chair that there would be a technician available. He would try to stop by for a lesson sometime before his class was ready to begin.

O'Neill decided to set up a workshop for the group of faculty who would be teaching on the system so that they would have an opportunity to get to know her and each other, learn about some of the unique aspects of distance teaching and the somewhat different characteristics of the distance learning audience, and find out how her office could assist them in preparing for their classes. Rather than sending them a formal invitation, she opted to drop by each of their offices, introduce herself, and invite them to the workshop personally. Dr. Johnson greeted her warmly, but he seemed distracted and unconvinced that the workshop was necessary or a good use of his time. She noticed he did not write down the time and place of the workshop, and in fact, he did not attend.

A few days later, O'Neill stood behind him in line at the deli and suggested they might visit about his upcoming class over lunch. He thanked her but indicated he was en route to a committee meeting. She also tried sending him an e-mail to schedule an appointment, but he did not respond. Finally, she sent him a letter with a few of the handouts she had used in the workshop to spark his interest. Again, he did not respond. Weeks went by as O'Neill worked with the other distance faculty in their pre-course planning, practice sessions, and adaptation of their visuals. She gradually became more concerned as the start of the semester drew near and Dr. Johnson continued to behave as if nothing were going to happen in his life. He appeared to remain confident that he would be able to walk into the distance classroom, teach as he normally does, and function fine without any help from O'Neill's office.

A few days before classes were to begin, the technical crew mentioned to O'Neill that Dr. Johnson had contacted them for a lesson on operating the classroom equipment and instructions on where to send his syllabus. The dean contacted her to let her know he and the president of the university were planning to sit in on a portion of Dr. Johnson's class, since it would be the first one to go "out" on the system. The technical crew notified her that they were having some minor technical problems with the audio in a couple of the remote sites. O'Neill decided she needed to forewarn Dr. Johnson about the coming events and offer to assist him in any last-minute planning or preparations. She phoned him to share the news. He thanked her for letting him know about the visitors and mentioned that he was going to get briefed on the classroom equipment that afternoon. She wished him well and told him that if he had any questions or concerns over the next few weeks, to feel free to contact her.

The next day, the excitement was palpable as Dr. Johnson's class time approached. O'Neill arrived early and waved at Dr. Johnson. He seemed a little anxious as the technical crew assisted him with the wireless microphone and reminded him about which monitor displayed the video signal being currently broadcast to the remote sites. A handful of students enrolled in the class at the host site filed in and sat scattered around the room. O'Neill waited for the dean and the president to arrive. Meanwhile, Dr. Johnson's department chair stopped by as well. Just as the class was to begin, the visitors arrived and moved into the back of the classroom.

Dr. Johnson began by introducing himself to the class and asking the class members to do so as well. He asked them to share their names and location and an experience each had with a K–12 classroom. He pulled out the printed list of registered students (40 in all across five sites) and called on Susan Anderson. She started talking but was difficult to hear. Dr. Johnson appeared a little flustered and asked her to speak up; although he could still not hear her well, he decided to move on and called the next name on his list. The next two students were seated in the host site. Dr. Johnson moved closer to them while they were talking but without realizing it, moved out of camera range. He dialogued a little with each student and then returned to the podium, where he worked his way through the list. A half hour crawled by as each student responded to the roll call; the host-site students appeared to pay little attention and became increasingly fidgety. Dr. Johnson gradually became aware that many of the students enrolled at the remote sites were older, working adults with lots of prior experience with K–12 education. Not only that, some sites had large numbers of students (many of whom he could hardly hear), while one site only had one student!

Next, Dr. Johnson decided he had better move on to discuss the syllabus if he were going to get to it before the class ended. He asked the remote-site students to locate the syllabus in their rooms while he passed them out to the host-site students. One of the students in Lawrenceville spoke up and said that there were no syllabi in the class materials box at his site. A second student at one of the other sites chimed in that there were none at her site either. Dr. Johnson looked anxiously at the technical staff, and then said that he would put the syllabus on the TV screen and look into what happened to the syllabi after class. (The dean leaned over to O'Neill and said, "This isn't going too well, is it?") Dr. Johnson placed the syllabi on the document camera, switched the control box so that the syllabi would be projected over the system, and zoomed in and out until he was comfortable with the size of the lettering on the monitor. Although the width of the syllabi was wider than the monitor now, he just moved it back and forth slightly as he read the document and explained portions of its content. Meanwhile, O'Neill hoped the dean was not aware of what was happening on the monitor screen. Zooming and moving the document was forcing the compressed video to redraw the screen often, giving the monitor an out-of-focus, swimming appearance most of the time.

Finally, Dr. Johnson decided to have the class form groups of five or six and brainstorm questions that they would like to see addressed during the course. He told everyone he would give them 10 minutes for the exercise, at which time they would be asked to share their list. As class time was running out, Dr. Johnson asked the Lawrenceville site to share their list first. After a moment's hesitation, one of the students there said that they had just managed to form their groups and needed more time to discuss the topic. At this point, Dr. Johnson took a look at the clock and decided to have the groups share their ideas at the beginning of the next class. O'Neill thought, "I am going to have to find a way to get faculty to want me to help them! How am I going to reach Dr. Johnson now?"

Invoking ID practice via the Kathryn O'Neill case

1. How is distance teaching similar to and different from traditional instruction? How do these factors impact faculty who are beginning to teach with the new medium?

2. How might the characteristics and needs of distance students be similar to, or different from, those of on-campus students? What kinds of instructional strategies, support services, or logistical practices might need to be implemented to serve them?

3. What are the primary concerns of the college dean and what responsibility does O'Neill have to meet them? Who are some of the other stakeholders in the new distance learning initiative?

4. Given Dr. Johnson's reluctance to accept assistance in preparing for his distance teaching assignment, what could O'Neill have done differently to win his cooperation? What is her responsibility in doing so? How can she sensitively use the new opportunity of "things not going well" to reach him now?

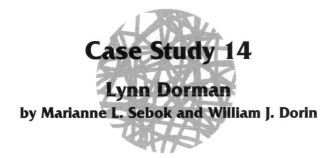

Case Study 14

Lynn Dorman

by Marianne L. Sebok and William J. Dorin

On a cold December morning in the Midwest, Lynn Dorman, newly graduated from a prestigious university with a master's degree in instructional design (ID), sipped a coffee in her four-wheel drive truck while on her way to work. One month before, she interviewed on campus with Roofing Industries; she was subsequently offered the position of instructional designer. This was her first day on the job, and she was both nervous and excited to meet the new challenges.

As Dorman continued her drive, she remembered the conversations she had with the production manager, Dave Okon, during her visit to the plant the previous week. Okon, a robust, bearded man in his fifties remarked how much "his people" need training; specifically, he cited the increase of employee accidents as cause for concern regarding plant training. Dorman began to think of potential reasons for the accident increase and discovered she was nearing the plant parking lot. She was amazed at the speed of her morning commute, partially due to her pre-occupation with her first major job assignment.

After Dorman unpacked supplies and began to settle in her new office later that morning, she began to review some of the materials Okon gave her at their last meeting. She studied two charts showing the amount and type of accidents over a six-month period a year apart (Figures 14.1 and 14.2). She could certainly see why the company was concerned with the rate of accidents; there seemed to be many more than expected.

As she was about to call Human Resources to ask about access to accident reports, Okon called and asked to meet with her on the shop floor. Dorman agreed to meet and put on the steel-toe shoes and hard hat required in the plant area. Although this was her second time in the plant area, she was impressed by the large noisy machines that created veritable canyons throughout. As she walked through the work areas, she noticed they were not well illuminated. She noticed the amount of dirt, dust, and grease that seemed to cover the floor and much of the machinery. A horn honk startled her as she moved out of the way of a forklift carrying a large skid of finished roofing shingles to the warehouse. She noticed the grease even more as she brushed her shop coat up against a packing machine. As she spotted Okon at the end of a long corridor, she took note of workers doing certain tasks with a routine rhythm. She was especially impressed with individuals placing the asphalt sheets on the press with such precise timing that it appeared effortless. In her short walk from her office to the meeting place with Okon, she felt that she was absorbing more information than she would be able to handle.

Okon's demeanor was cordial yet firm; he was concerned about his employees and would like them to take a required training course dealing with the fundamental aspects of plant/machine safety. "Even some of the old timers need training," he responded with a slight grin. He further explained the new advances in computer technology recently undertaken by Roofing Industries. Primarily, the new computer programs focus on quality control specifications and require employees to conduct random sampling of products. These samples are used to determine if quality specifications match customer orders. Such controls were new innovations that had been installed within the previous several months.

In addition to mentioning the new computer controls, Okon stated that production speed had increased considerably during the previous six months. "Due to customer demand, we have had to increase our line speed; a lot of our people have been angry they have to work harder. Some of my people don't realize they are getting careless while they are working. Now that I think about it, it seems like a lot of the old timers have trouble trying to keep up with the new pace. I'm sure some training would help all my employees."

Dorman mentioned that she had started to look at the data just before Okon called her. She asked him if he could give some specifics about the different types of accidents. As he looked down the rows of machines, he motioned for her to follow him. He stopped at one of the presses that was down and told her how one man was injured when he failed to use the rake to pull some roofing sheets forward. Okon described how the guy reached in to the press and did not notice the hot tar dripping down.

"Bad enough he reaches into a 2000-pound press, but it was the hot tar that gave him third degree burns on his arm. He wasn't wearing the long-sleeve elbow guards," said Okon. Dorman bent over to look under the press and saw the now-cooled dry tar and roofing material. Okon motioned to her again and they walked to the raw materials area. Here Dorman saw workers pulling packing crates and boxes apart with knives, hammers, shears, and crowbars. She noticed immediately how a steel band would recoil when someone cut it off the box.

She also noticed how the staples would fly around when pulled out with the crowbars. She paid attention to how the workers were dressed and turned to Okon with a question.

"What type of injuries happen here?" she asked. Okon told her it was mostly small abrasions, cuts, and getting material in the eyes. "Don't you make these guys wear gloves and goggles doing this job?" Dorman asked. Okon said it was policy, and workers could get written up if they were injured, but many of them complained they could not work quickly while wearing gloves. He added that most of the workers did wear their goggles on windy days when dust was really flying around. Just then Okon's pager sounded, and he abruptly left Dorman as he answered his call. Dorman stood watching for a few more minutes and then headed back to her office.

Later in the privacy of her office, she jotted down the mental notes she had compiled during her discussion with Okon. Subsequently, she made other notations about the facts surrounding this situation:

▶ Approximately 500 employees work in the roofing plant, 60% of the employees have been on the job for more than 10 years; 95% have high school diplomas and are able to read and speak English.

▶ Categories of employees include: production manager (1), shift supervisors (14), production employees (460), cleaning crew staff (20), and office staff including clerical, instructional designer, office manager, accounting manager, and human resources personnel (9).

▶ Production operates on two shifts: 7:00 A.M.–3:30 P.M. and 4:00 P.M.–12:30 A.M.; cleaning crew: 12:00 A.M.–8:30 A.M. (All employees receive two 15-minute breaks and a 30-minute lunch/dinner break.)

▶ Most accidents originate from the production employees, although cleaning crew staff do have accidents from time to time.

▶ The budget for a potential needs assessment has been designated at $1000 (including materials and possible downtime associated with production).

▶ Should a needs assessment occur, the production manager stated it must be completed within 30–45 days. The production manager believes in and supports training initiatives; however, downtime and scheduling should be kept to a minimum.

Given these facts, Dorman must decide how to best proceed. What data should she collect? How can she collect the data that she needs? Can she manage to collect all the information she needs within the time frame imposed by management? Will she have sufficient access to factory personnel and activities to effectively assess the situation? Dorman pondered all these questions as she made her way back to her office. She had heard and seen a lot on her first morning, and now she wondered if she could make sense of it all.

Invoking ID practice via the Lynn Dorman case

1. Describe information Dorman currently has. What further information does she need to obtain?
2. Suggest appropriate needs assessment strategies for this situation.
3. Propose appropriate information gathering instruments and develop the principal elements of each recommended instrument.
4. Develop a timeline for the entire needs assessment process.

Figure 14.1   Roofing Industry Accidents One Year Ago

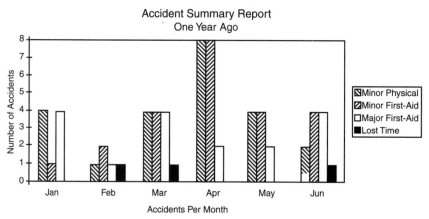

Figure 14.2   Roofing Industry Accidents in the Current Six Months

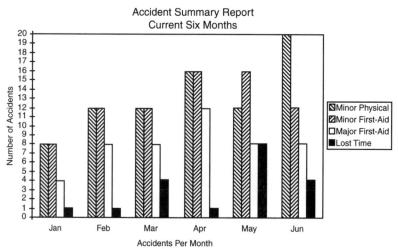

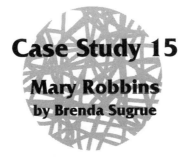

Case Study 15

Mary Robbins
by Brenda Sugrue

The Cuts-R-Us hairdressing school hired Asgard Training to redesign its entry-level course. The famous hair stylist, Hugo, has always been responsible for this course. The course lasts 12 weeks and covers the basics of cutting and coloring. Twenty students take the course at one time and the course is run three times a year. The reason that the consulting company was hired was that usually 50 percent of students who begin the course do not finish. The positive consequence of the high "failure" rate is that the course is regarded as one of the best in the country. The negative consequences are that (1) the company only makes half of the money it could make on this course since it refunds tuition fees to anyone who does not complete the course, and (2) there are fewer students for the advanced courses that the school offers. Cuts-R-Us wants to increase its "graduation rate" from the basic course. The director also believes that they could run more than three basic courses per year and if the course were better documented, instructors other than Hugo could teach it.

Mary Robbins from Asgard Training conducted a needs analysis and came to the conclusion that the existing course materials were incomplete, disorganized, and badly sequenced. The course content was mostly inside Hugo's head and he covered topics in whatever order he wished. Robbins recommended that a thorough cognitive task analysis be done using Hugo as the expert, and that a set of print-based job aids (laminated cards in a notebook-size looseleaf binder) be created for each technique that trainees would learn. Each week would focus on one cutting and one coloring technique, beginning with the simplest techniques. She convinced Hugo that the basic strategy for teaching each technique would be a demonstration of the technique by him and many opportunities for the trainees to practice the technique and get feedback on their progress. Since Hugo could not personally monitor all of the practice, it was decided to group students in pairs and have one person practice while the other would coach, switching roles back and forth. Every Friday, each student would be videotaped performing the techniques of the week and Hugo would assign pass or fail grades to each student for the week based on his viewing of the videotapes. If a student fails three weeks in a row, then he or she must drop the course. In addition, it was decided to pretest all students on their level of fluid ability (generally conceived of as novel problem-solving ability and often measured by tests of noverbal reasoning), because this is known to be a good indicator of the amount of structure and feedback a student will need during instruction.

Robbins will carefully monitor the first offering of the new course in order to make adjustments during the course and to make revisions for future offerings. Part of this "formative" evaluation involves tape recording conversations among groups of students who are taking the course.

▶ Relevant Data

This case will focus on four students (Roberto, Philip, Donna, and Krystal) enrolled in the first offering of the new course. What follows are two conversations that take place among these four students. The first conversation takes place on the first day of the course; the second conversation takes place at the beginning of the fifth week of the course.

▶ The Case

Week 1

Roberto:

So, are you guys looking forward to this?

Krystal:

Of course. I can't wait to get started. I've always wanted to be a hairdresser and I can't believe that they accepted me into the program with my low high school GPA. School was so tough for me… all that reading and writing… but I'm really good with hair; I worked part time in a salon last year. I spent all my time just washing hair, but the cutting and coloring seems just as easy. I don't even know why we have to train for three months. But at least it's a break from real work. I'm going to treat it like a vacation. How about you?

Roberto:

Well, I'm a bit nervous myself. I hear that it's kind of like a boot camp here and if you don't pass the weekly tests, they throw you out. And they don't give you much help. But the good thing is that if you train here, you can get a job in any salon; this is supposed to be one of the best hairdressing schools in the country. You know, Tony Ronato, the guy who cuts the president's hair, trained here.

Philip:

Yeah, but he then went off to France and worked with Pierre LeBlanc; that's where he really got trained. You won't get a good job with just this course. I wanted to go to the Sidel Academy but didn't get in, so this is a last resort for me, and if I could go right into a salon without it, that's what I'd do. But unfortunately, all salons require some basic training and so I'll suffer through this. But I can't wait for it to be over.

Donna:

Me too, I already know all this stuff; I've been working at my dad's salon for a year now, doing everything, cutting, coloring, perming, the lot. My dad's Frederiko. But I want to open my own salon and you have to have a certificate and this school was the quickest way I can get that. What a drag.

Roberto:

Wow, you're Frederiko's daughter! Do you think I could meet him? He's my all-time hero. I just love the way he did Liz's shaggy cut.

Philip:

What did you think of them making us take that stupid "pick the next picture in the series" test on the computer this morning? They said it was some kind of fancy IQ test. I'm glad that they gave us our scores right away. I got 90 percent!! I wish I could show that to my old high school teachers. They thought I was dumb because I never did any work and always failed their silly tests. But I knew I was smart all along.

Roberto:

Well, I only got 60 percent. I was confused when the patterns got so complicated. I hope that doesn't mean they'll be watching me closely all the time. How smart do you have to be to cut hair anyway? And what does picture matching have to do with cutting hair?

Donna:

I agree. I think that they were just trying to scare us. I only got 65 on the test this morning and I've been doing great cuts at my dad's salon.

Krystal:

Well, I liked the test. You didn't have to study for it, just figure out the patterns. I got 85 and I could have done better if I hadn't been distracted by that gorgeous looking guy sitting in front of me.

Week 5

At the beginning of the fifth week of their training, Roberto has failed weeks 3 and 4. Donna and Krystal failed week 4. Philip has passed in all four weeks. Roberto and Donna have been working together as a pair. Krystal and Philip have also been a pair.

Roberto:

I don't know what I'm going to do. If I fail this week, I'm out. I wish I could ask Hugo for help, but he's so impatient and I'm scared he'll think I'm even worse than I am. I'm trying so hard. I was doing fine the first two weeks, when we were doing basic trims and layering. But the coloring is so hard...matching the chemicals to the customer's hair, and getting the time right. I felt so bad for that woman when her hair came out green. I wonder if I could hire my own tutor. Donna, you're great, but you don't tell me what I'm doing wrong, and last week, your own coloring was a disaster.

Donna:

Now, listen here, Roberto, I'm not here to teach you. You're just holding me back. I wouldn't have failed last week if you hadn't been watching me like a hawk and telling me I was doing things wrong when they were right! I wish I could just work on my own.

Philip:

I don't know what your problem is, Roberto. It shows you exactly what to do in the manual. It even has pictures of what a cut or color should look like at every stage. When I'm watching Krystal, I put an X beside each step she does that does not match the picture in the book, and then show it to her after. Roberto, if you like, I'll help you in the evenings this week. We can practice on some cheap wigs.

Krystal:

Roberto, if you let Philip help you, you'll pass this week. Philip is almost as good as Hugo, and much more patient. Philip, if it wasn't for you, I'd have failed every week. The only reason I failed last week was because of that terrible woman I had to work on for the video. She kept telling me what to do with her hair, so that I couldn't practice what we were supposed to be practicing. It's so unfair. And so much work. We can't relax for a minute. If I'd known the training was going to be this hard, I might not have enrolled.

Roberto:

Thanks, Philip. There may be hope for me after all.

Philip:

Of course there's hope. They're packing a lot into 12 weeks, that's why you're having trouble. But I like it this way. I'm glad that they leave us alone most of the time. And I like having a partner too. I'm a lot happier than I expected to be when I started. Hugo says I'm one of the best students he's ever had!

Donna:

Just because you're always asking questions and showing off. Just wait until I have my own salon and am inventing new styles, like my dad. I hate the boring old styles they are making us learn here; they are so eighties. And they make it all seem so complicated. I'm not going to remember any of their stupid rules anyway. I'll do what it takes to get the certificate, but then I'll wipe it all from my mind and go back to the way I was doing things before I came.

Roberto:

But Hugo says that all new styles are just variations on the basics, and that you have to know the basic rules before you try experimenting.

Donna:

But hairdressing is about experimenting, not about sticking to rules. I feel stifled with all these rules and steps.

Philip:

Well, you'll never have your own salon if you don't pass this course.

Donna:

There are plenty of other training programs. If I don't pass this one, I'll just enroll somewhere else, somewhere where they value my creative talent and don't make me learn all this stupid stuff.

Invoking ID practice via the Mary Robbins case

1. Create a profile of the abilities and motivational characteristics of each of the four learners in the case at the beginning of the training course and one month later.

2. Discuss what kinds of data can be used as indicators of ability and motivation before and during instruction.

3. Identify matches and mismatches between the training as designed and the four learners in the case.

4. Identify the key source of poor performance for each of the three learners who are failing.

5. Discuss micro and macro adaptations to the training so that all four learners will succeed.

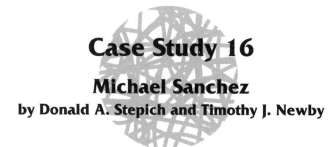

Case Study 16

Michael Sanchez

by Donald A. Stepich and Timothy J. Newby

Michael Sanchez, training project manager for Universal Electronics, a large consumer electronics manufacturing company, left his boss's office with a new assignment. Suzanne Manning, Universal's training director, had asked, "Can you show that 'Differences' is really making a difference to the company?" "Differences Among People" ("Differences" for short) is the company's diversity training program. If this course is going to stay on the books, and Manning thinks it should, now is the time to demonstrate its value because next year's training budget is being considered. The company is looking to cut unnecessary courses and this course may be on the chopping block. This is a different kind of project for Sanchez. He's helped design a large number of training programs, but this is the first time he's done this kind of evaluation project.

Manning had explained that Universal's management has been taking a more critical look at training, challenging the value of every training course. It isn't that management doesn't believe in training. Over the years the company has invested heavily in training and there are no signs that this investment will be reduced any time soon. However, just as with new marketing strategies or manufacturing techniques, management wants to see tangible evidence that a particular training course is working to the company's benefit. They want to be able to base their decision on information rather than opinion. So far, the emphasis has been on technical training (for example, courses on engineering standards and quality control methods), and some courses have been eliminated or substantially revised. However, the focus has been shifting to the "soft skills" courses (for example, courses on teamwork and coaching skills), which present a more difficult problem.

Manning's opinion was that "Differences" was valuable when it was first offered and is still valuable today. Curriculum decisions were being made in 60 to 90 days, and she would have to make a recommendation about this course and back that recommendation up. If the course is still valuable, she would need more than her opinion to convince management to keep it on the books for the next year. She'd need some hard evidence. And if the course is no longer valuable, then maybe it was time to scrap it. Sanchez knew that this, too, would require hard evidence. He knew Manning well enough to know that, regardless of the situation, she liked to be thorough in backing up her recommendations. He also remembered that she had been one of the initial promoters of the course. She worked hard to get "Differences" going in the organization. He knew that she wouldn't recommend dropping this course lightly. Either way, Sanchez knew that whether the employees learned anything wasn't really the issue. For the evaluation to be useful, he would have to find out whether what they learned was having a positive effect on the company as a whole.

Sanchez had asked about the original purpose for the course. It had started out as a "bandwagon" course. Especially with the passage of the Americans with Disabilities Act (ADA), it seemed like everyone was doing diversity training, and Universal's management saw this course as a way to "keep up with the Joneses." In addition, while the company hadn't been in any legal trouble, management wanted to keep it that way. The course was designed to show that the company was treating all of its employees in a fair and equitable way and encouraging them to treat one another in the same way. The expectation was that this would help keep the company out of court, or at least lessen the impact of any lawsuit. Sanchez thought there were significant problems with these arguments. Diversity didn't seem to be the hot topic it had been a year or two ago, so the bandwagon argument wouldn't carry the same weight. The legal argument was still valid but seemed relatively weak because it was presented in negative terms—avoiding lawsuits. To assess the value of the course, Sanchez thought it would be important to approach it from a positive perspective—to determine whether the course was having a positive effect, rather than simply helping to avoid a negative effect.

After some thought, he came up with two approaches that he thought would work. The "employee development" approach was based on the fact that, because of Affirmative Action (AA) and Equal Employment Opportunity (EEO) guidelines, the company had been hiring and promoting an increasing number of women and minorities. A substantial investment had been made in these employees, an investment the company would want to protect. The argument was that if employees (all employees) better understood their unique backgrounds and perspectives, then these minority and women employees might have a better chance of succeeding on the job. As a result, they might be more likely to want to stay with the company, giving the company a greater return on the investment it had made in them.

The "productivity" approach was based on the fact that consumer electronics is a very competitive business. Innovation and productivity were critical to the company's continued success in the market. The argument was that the more employees understood about one another, the easier it would be for them to communicate with one another, which would result in better problem solving. As a result, both innovation and productivity would increase, helping the company maintain a competitive edge in the market.

Sanchez reviewed the course materials. "Differences" is a two-day course designed to improve the communication among the company's employees by making them more aware of the ways communication is influenced by the age, gender, and cultural background of the people involved. The course attempts to accomplish this by teaching some basic listening and conflict resolution skills, providing information about the common differences among different age, gender, and cultural groups, and describing the impact stereotyping has on communication between groups. The course format includes a combination of lectures, videos, discussions, self-assessment exercises, and experiential activities. Response to the course has been generally positive. Based on course evaluations completed at the end of every training course, employees seem to feel that the information in "Differences" is interesting, clearly presented, and useful.

Invoking ID practice via the Michael Sanchez case

1. Identify the key issues from both the management and training department's perspectives.

2. Develop a list of indicators of "employee development" (e.g., What are employees doing differently?) and "productivity" (e.g., How is this affecting the company's performance?).

3. Develop a plan for obtaining information related to the "employee development" and "productivity" approaches.

4. Discuss the relative value of both approaches from management's point of view.

5. Identify Sanchez's dilemma in this situation. What is Manning's attitude toward the training program? How might her attitude affect Sanchez's evaluation?

Case Study 17
Michelle Nguyen
by Joanna C. Dunlap

Michelle Nguyen came to work on Monday morning feeling optimistic and looking forward to the week's work ahead. Walking into her office, she looked at the project Gantt charts that covered one whole wall. She smiled as she reexamined the timeline for the hematology computer-based instructional (CBI) project she had been working on for the last nine months. Although there had been some delays throughout the project due to the complexity of the content and the design, as well as the busy schedules of the two physicians functioning as subject-matter experts on the project, Nguyen had been able to keep the project within budget and on schedule, a fact of which she was very proud! Having completed the formative evaluation and made the necessary changes, she was ready to begin implementing the program for student use—just in time for the spring semester.

The product Nguyen was implementing was a CBI program on hematology for third-year medical students. The program would replace an existing classroom-based course covering such topics as hazards of giving and receiving blood products, indications for transfusion, transfusion products, and the diagnosis and treatment of diseases that impact blood production and functioning. Developed as part of a medical education grant, the program was the medical school's first big CBI program and was, therefore, designed to be the flagship in a line of proposed CBI programs to be integrated into the third-year curriculum. Instructors and administrators had expressed some healthy skepticism regarding the quality of the learning experience in a CBI environment and the strain on scarce instructional resources that CBI projects can have, so Nguyen had taken it upon herself to make sure that the program alleviated those concerns and came to market without a hitch.

Ever since she took the project over nine months ago she had been looking forward to getting the program online. She had accomplished a lot during the course of this project. Although it was not the first time she had developed computer-based instruction, it was the first time she had used constructivist instructional methodologies to structure the CBI. Not only was she utilizing new instructional methodologies, Nguyen was also a novice when it came to the content domain of hematology. She was far from being a hematologist and, therefore, had to rely extensively on the subject-matter experts assigned to the project. Her skills at mining for knowledge from subject-matter experts were constantly challenged; the two physicians acting as experts were enthusiastic about the project but had trouble expressing their expertise and their decision-making processes in ways that would be appropriate for instructing third-year medical students. In addition, the physicians' schedules were almost prohibitive, especially given that Nguyen worked from 8:00 to 5:00, during which time the physicians were busy teaching, conducting research, working with patients, running a blood center, as well as being on call for the hospital. And, if that wasn't enough, Nguyen had also spent nine months listening to the physicians' "Dr. Stab" jokes and, whenever they noticed her getting squeamish, being subjected to their detailed descriptions of their own medical school experiences, such as bumping into cadavers in dark hallways and the unexpected surprises that can occur during an autopsy.

The project had required her to do a lot of work in a short time with a limited budget, dealing with sophisticated subject-matter experts and applying complex instructional methodologies to an ill-structured content domain using computer technology as a delivery vehicle. Thinking about how it was almost over, she mimed wiping her brow with her hand. Nguyen was proud of her work and knew that once the program was implemented and the students were actually using it, the hematology program was going to be a feather in her cap! Still smiling, she walked to her desk to answer the ringing telephone.

"Hello. Instructional Technology Department. This is Michelle."

"Hey, Michelle. This is Tom DiBona over in Academic Computing. Are you sitting down? We've got a problem. . . ."

▶ Nine months ago

After being assigned to the new hematology CBI development project, Nguyen set up a meeting with the project's feasibility team—the people who had developed the original grant proposal. Alex Wheeler and Susan Martin had conducted a front-end analysis for this project as part of the initial grant proposal; the front-end analysis, in fact, helped sell the project to the selection committee and secured the award. Nguyen had some information: the new hematology course had to be "real world," CBI, self-guided, and something that students could easily access given their busy clerkship schedules. Before she began work on the design of the product, she wanted to meet with Wheeler and Martin to go over how their front-end analysis recommendations were derived so she would fully understand what the final product needed to be. From experience, Nguyen knew that regardless of how instructionally sound or innovative her design was, the program would fail to be an effective instructional tool if the front-end analysis recommendations were not reflected in the final product.

After Nguyen, Wheeler, and Martin were settled in the conference room, Nguyen asked them to describe the instructional motivation for the project. Wheeler started the discussion by talking about why the hematology course needed redesigning. Their findings indicated that the current hematology course was failing to meet the needs of the students for three reasons:

1. The hematology content was delivered in a classroom setting via lecture. These lectures took place during the day to fit into the professors' work schedules. However, the students' clerkship schedules required them to be at their assigned hospital or clinic during the day. Therefore, it was difficult for students to attend lectures; students needed an instructional intervention that they could access during hours not spent in their clerkships.

2. Now that they were in their clerkships, the students did not see the relevance of the hematology content, especially since it was presented in a decontextualized way. That is, the content was usually presented by professors using a lecture format—defining concept after concept in sequence, prototypically, simplistically, and in isolation. Under these conditions students failed to learn how hematology related to other medical content domains or how it impacted the decisions doctors make on the job.

3. Students were so stressed about being in their clerkships that the last thing they wanted to do was "learn more content." Martin described the problem to Nguyen in the following way:

    As you know, Michelle, this medical school is really no different from most. Our students begin their clerkships during the third year. Suddenly, students who are really good at taking lecture notes, studying textbooks, and passing exams are required to perform tasks they haven't practiced. They're required to use all of the facts they have memorized in biology, pathophysiology, chemistry, anatomy and so on in an interdisciplinary way to solve a real patient's real-world, real-time problem … a leap that is very stressful and not always successful for students who've never been asked to perform that way and have never had a chance to practice.

The rest of the information Wheeler and Martin provided Nguyen had to do with environmental issues that would impact her design:

▶ Students needed to be able to use the program in the library's academic computing labs.

▶ The library's computer resources consisted of Macintosh computers networked to laser printers.

▶ Students were fairly computer literate, using word processing and on-line reference search tools.

Using her notes from her meeting with Wheeler, and Martin, Nguyen made the following design decisions for the hematology program:

▶ According to the front-end analysis, Nguyen needed to create a program that would not only cover the appropriate hematology content but that would also help "bridge the gap" between what and how students learn in a conventional medical school environment and how they were expected to function and apply their knowledge and skills to a medical emergency in a hospital setting. To do this, the program would be a case-based instructional environment that would enable students to practice applying what they have learned in the classroom to solving real problems, in a safe, nonthreatening environment. Using appropriate instructional methodologies, Nguyen knew she could develop a structure for presenting hematology cases that encouraged students to think, research, problem-solve, and ultimately make the types of decisions regarding hematology issues they would be making in their clerkships. This would address the issues of relevance and practice brought up during the front-end analysis.

▶ The program would be self-guided and self-contained so students could access the instruction when it fit into their busy schedules. This would address the time constraint issue students had with the classroom-based hematology course.

Using these macro-level design decisions to guide her work, Nguyen worked with the subject-matter experts to develop a CBI product that fulfilled the requirements of the front-end analysis conducted by Wheeler and Martin.

▶ Today

"What do you mean, Tom?"

"Well, Michelle, I've been going over the results of the academic computing needs survey we've been having students fill out over the last four weeks. We've had a really good response . . . 65 percent so far. What I'm worried about is that the students have indicated that the library's hours are not sufficient; specifically, the third- and fourth-year students are saying they are working in their clerkships during library hours and, therefore, need us to have extended hours. So, if you're planning on using the library's computer labs for the hematology program, you're going to have an access problem for the third-year students."

"But, Tom, hold on. When I took over this project, I met with Alex and Susan to go over the front-end analysis for this project. Their data indicated that making it available in the library was the best solution. I don't—"

"Michelle. That front-end analysis was conducted over a year ago. Last year we had the budget to hire folks to keep the library open after hours. With the new fiscal year, that budget was cut. No more extended hours. Alex and Susan know this—haven't you been meeting with them throughout your project to make sure the original front-end analysis data was still on target?"

Nguyen was silent, feeling paralyzed by the news. "No, not really." As DiBona continued to describe what the students were writing on the survey, Nguyen pulled her file on the academic computing needs survey to review the questions for herself.

"OK. Tom, what if—if we can't provide library access for students to use the program, what about making the program available for home use? Don't most of our students have computers at home? Didn't I see a question on the survey that gets at this?"

"Yes, Michelle, that's covered in questions 3 through 6 on the survey. But you know that anything related to computer technology can change overnight. Those students that didn't have a clue how to use the Internet are now on the Web constantly. But here's the rest of the bad news. The majority of our students do have access to computers at home. But they have PCs, not Macintoshes. I don't suppose it's easy to convert your program to run on a PC platform? "

Staring at the front-end analysis report on which she had based many of her design, development, and implementation decisions, Nguyen examined the data summary for questions 3 through 6 (Figure 17.1).

Figure 17.1   Data Summary

		Yes	No
3)	**Do you know how to use a:**		
	Macintosh computer?	711	223
	Windows computer?	587	336
	printer?	806	137
	CD-ROM?	254	539
	modem?	223	647
4)	**Do you have access to a computer at:**		
	home?	519	314
	work?	475	588
5)	**What software applications do you use:**		
	word processing?	847	166
	database?	154	779
	presentation?	127	857
	spreadsheet?	188	736
	Internet/World Wide Web?	285	566
	MedLine?	247	619
6)	**Do you use a computer to:**		
	write papers?	687	156
	conduct research?	263	658
	deliver presentations?	127	684

For the first time, she realized that the survey did not ask for enough detail regarding computer platform and home availability. The rest of her conversation with DiBona was a blur. The project was now in trouble and if she wanted to make sure it was available for the spring semester as promised, she needed an immediate solution. Pulling the project files from the filing cabinet, Nguyen asked herself how this could happen to her "perfect" project. She had done everything by the book, using the front-end analysis findings to guide her design decisions. She had paid especially close attention to the environmental analysis results: access, platform, and so on. How could she get to the implementation phase of the project and suddenly have all these problems? How would this set back impact the project's budget, resource needs, quality, and timeline? Nguyen closed her office door, forwarded her phone, and began to think about how she might salvage her project.

Invoking ID practice via the Michelle Nguyen case

1. Identify the key issues in the case.
2. Describe the relationship among the front-end analysis, design, and implementation phases of the instructional development project described in this case.
3. Discuss the appropriateness of Nguyen's ID decisions.
4. Evaluate Nguyen's actions and identify what she might have done differently.
5. Discuss what actions you could take to avoid problems during implementation.
6. Describe a scenario in which a project is taken from analysis through implementation with no surprises. Present a rationale for your recommended procedures.

Case Study 18

Rebekka Chapman
by Sara Jane Coffman

Monday morning. I was sitting in my office at the Faculty Instructional Services Center, trying to catch up on some paperwork, when the phone rang. George Allen, a department head on campus, explained he'd just had a group of students in his office complaining about their instructor. Tami Linden was new to campus and rather "strong-willed." The class was EXTREMELY upset with her. He didn't think he'd have much luck getting this instructor to change her teaching style (even though it was mid-semester and an ideal time to make changes) so he asked if I'd call her and offer my assistance.

It had never worked in the past for me to call an instructor and say, "Listen, you don't know me, but I hear you're having some trouble with your class." So I told the department head I'd be happy to work with her, but only if she initiated the request.

I could tell he didn't relish going back to this "strong-willed" woman and suggest she call an instructional developer for help with her course. I figured that was the last I'd hear about it.

Much to my surprise, within the next few minutes, the phone rang again. It was the alleged "strong-willed" instructor asking for help with her teaching. She was surprisingly friendly. (Did this indicate a problem between her and her department head?) She said that she would love to talk to me; she was feeling frustrated and discouraged that students from her class had gone to the department head to complain. She thought her class was going fairly well. We scheduled a meeting in her office that afternoon.

Because it sounded like an interesting case, I asked a colleague to come along. Maybe there would be an advantage to getting two views on the situation. It sounded like this class was on fire and that this instructor could use all the help she could get.

Tami Linden had an interesting office. Lenny and I sat on little futons that were inches off the ground, while Tami loomed way above us in a regulation-sized chair. She offered us soft drinks from a refrigerator she'd brought into the office. We finished our drinks way before Tami was finished talking about her class.

Tami was short and had bright red hair. She had just graduated with her Ph.D. from a school on the East Coast two weeks before the semester began. At age 40, she'd also recently gotten married and moved to campus. Needless to say, her life had been stressful lately. But she explained that she had been thoroughly looking forward to teaching at the university—this is what she'd wanted to do for a long time. She was thrilled to be at such a prestigious university. Even though she'd had little time to put together her course syllabus, it looked clear and solid. It was a required consumer retailing course with over 100 juniors and seniors.

"Uh oh," I thought. I hated it when department heads put brand-new people in such large classes for their first teaching assignment.

After listening to her, it seemed that the students and instructor had a lack of respect for each other. The students were very upset about their grades. They thought they were being graded too harshly. They also didn't understand why they had to do so many writing assignments—about one per week. The reason, according to Tami, was because they'd be writing on their jobs, which were just a year or two away. Their level of writing was appalling, as far as Tami was concerned. She was extremely committed to the writing assignments. Where else were they going to learn to write well before they graduated? It was impressive to see how much feedback she was giving her students on their papers. Their papers were due on Fridays and she would spend the entire weekend grading them.

"What a way to spend weekends—especially as a newlywed," I thought.

On the positive side, their writing *was* improving. Tami was very encouraged by the learning that was occurring. This is why she thought everything was going so well.

Lenny and I began by giving her suggestions to regain the students' respect. We encouraged her to dress more formally and to teach from behind the podium. Lenny especially encouraged her to share articles with her class from people in the field of consumer retailing, explaining the importance of being able to write. I also offered to sit in her class the next day.

I came away from our first meeting unsure of who owned this problem. Were the students—who'd been in classes with each other and who had a good relationship with the department head—ganging up on a new instructor so they could get higher grades with less work? Or was Tami, whose faster and more abrupt communication style (typical of the East Coast, but uncommon in the Midwest), to blame?

When I sat in Tami's class the next day, I noticed that she was giving off all sorts of signals that she wanted her students to like her—she kept coming out into the center aisle, leaning in toward them, and engaging them in questions. But when students answered, they used it as an opportunity to overtly challenge her and/or talk about her under their breath. My impression was, if she were going to salvage things, she needed to assert more authority: Lecture more, stop asking questions.

The content of the lecture seemed fine to me, so I asked Tami if I could conduct a Small Group Instructional Diagnosis (SGID) to find out what the class was thinking. SGID is a course/instructor evaluation technique where an outside facilitator elicits feedback (based on group consensus) about what students like about a course and what suggestions they have for improving it.

This was agreeable to Tami. I conducted the SGID the next class period. The results revealed the following suggestions:

1. Fewer writing assignments.
2. More directions on assignments.
3. Clarify the point system.
4. Let us see the test average.
5. Better review for exam.
6. Stop teaching straight from the book and use more discussion.
7. Better organization.
8. Treat us more like adults.
9. Get happy.
10. Get rid of this instructor.

After I had conducted the evaluation, several students came up to me and explained that they didn't see why they had to do writing assignments in this class. They'd already earned "A's" in English 101 in their freshman year and felt Dr. Linden had no business grading them on their writing. So here was a good teaching goal—to improve their writing—certainly not being appreciated by the students. The students also mentioned that they didn't have to write in *any* of their other classes in this department.

This was probably a big part of the problem. It's always hard to introduce a new teaching technique into a department—especially if you're a newcomer.

Invoking ID practice via the Rebekka Chapman case

1. Identify the problem(s) Tami is currently facing in her class.
2. Discuss these problems from both the students' and the professor's point of view.
3. Discuss strategies for implementing new activities and requirements in an established course, including gaining support from stakeholders.
4. Suggest possible changes in course design and implementation in response to student evaluations.
5. Discuss intervention strategies for salvaging a poor beginning to a course. Provide a rationale for recommended strategies.
6. Describe strategies for implementing effective class discussions in a large class.

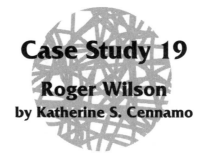

Case Study 19

Roger Wilson
by Katherine S. Cennamo

Roger Wilson was asked to design and develop an introduction to the Logo programming language for inclusion in an "Introductory Computing" class for preservice elementary teachers. Although the course instructor realized that the students may need a working knowledge of Logo as elementary teachers, he could allocate only one 2 1/2-hour class period to the topic. After talking with the course instructor and current students in the course, Wilson developed objectives, test items, and an instructional strategy to teach students to create a complex geometric figure using Logo. He decided to create a print-based "workbook" that students could complete for homework. By doing workbook activities, they would learn to use the PU, PD, RT, LF, FD, and REPEAT commands (see Figure 19.1 for the Instructional Analysis of objectives). The instructor planned to build on this core knowledge during his class session and accompanying lab session. We join Wilson near the end of the systematic instructional design process—during formative evaluation of his Logo workbook.

▶ One-on-One Evaluations

Wilson conducted three one-on-one evaluations with student evaluators who closely resembled the target population. "Student A" was enrolled in the "Introductory Computing" class; however, her grades were below average and she often missed class. "Student B" was a student assistant in the computer lab. He was proficient in computer use but had no prior knowledge of programming in Logo. Because he would be expected to help other students with Logo projects, he was very motivated to learn the language. "Student C" also was employed by the computer lab. She was responsible for collecting student identification cards at the front desk. Though she had never used a computer before, she appeared to learn quickly.

During the one-on-one evaluation sessions, the students were told that they would be trying out some new materials to identify areas that needed improvement. They were encouraged to ask questions or make

Figure 19.1 Instructional Analysis

GOAL: Given a diagram of complex geometric figure, the student will list the procedures that would result in a similar output using the PU, PD, RT, LF, FD, and REPEAT commands of the LOGO language.

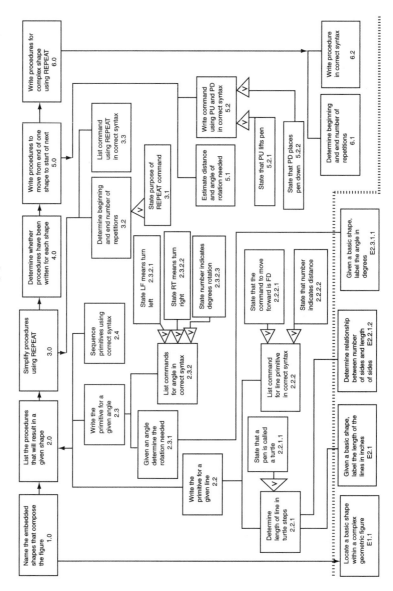

suggestions at any time. All three seemed interested in assisting in the revision of the materials.

Wilson and the students had identical sets of instructional materials. Each student freely expressed their concerns, questions, uncertainties, and comments; Wilson made notes directly on his set of materials.

All the students successfully completed the workbook, acomplishing the tasks they were expected to accomplish. However, Wilson did provide clarification at certain points in the instruction. Since the workbooks were intended to be self-instructional homework activities, he made the following modifications based on the results of the one-on-one evaluations:

▶ Modified instructions and questions for the pretest, posttest, and practice items

▶ Altered several illustrations for clarity

▶ Added several other illustrations for models and reference

▶ Added a summary to the end of the lesson

▶ Small-Group Evaluation

Next, Wilson conducted a small-group evaluation with eight students currently enrolled in the class. The instructor agreed to allow eight volunteers to leave the class for the small-group evaluation, while remaining class members received information on the same topic in a lecture/lab format. Five females and three males participated in the evaluation.

The evaluations were conducted in a group setting. The participants were taken to a quiet conference room and seated at three long tables. There was a large clock on the wall above the tables. Wilson explained that the purpose of the session was to evaluate the instructional materials. He instructed the students to fill in all the blanks in the workbook and to record the time they started and finished each activity.

He began the instruction by administering a pretest. Students were struggling to complete the pretest until he assured them that they were not expected to know all the answers yet. After completing the pretest, the students were given a packet that contained the workbook and the posttest. Each student completed these materials independently. After they finished the posttest, Wilson collected the materials and asked each student to complete an attitude questionnaire. By this point, the students were frustrated with the excessive time spent on the instructional materials, but each reluctantly agreed to complete the questionnaire.

The next day, Wilson scored the pretests, embedded practice activities, and posttests. He summarized the students' scores for entry skills, pretest, and posttest by higher-level objectives (see Figures 19.2 to 19.4).

Figure 19.2 Students Mastering Objectives for Entry Skills

		E1.1	E2.1	E2.3.1.1	E2.2.1.2
	A	1			1
	B	1	1	1	1
	C	1	1	1	1
Students	D	0	1		0
	E	1	0	1	1
	F	1	1	0	1
	G	1	1	1	1
	H	1	1	1	1
	% of Mastery	87.0%	85.7%	83.3%	87.0%

Objectives

Key to coding: Blank — no response
0 — nonmastery
1 — mastery

Figure 19.3 Students Mastering Objectives on Pretest

		1.0	2.0	3.0	4.0	5.0	6.0
	A	1	0	0	0	0	0
	B	1	0	0	0	0	0
	C	1	0	0	0	0	0
Students	D	1	0	0	0	0	0
	E	1	0	0	0	0	0
	F	1	0	0	0	0	0
	G	1	0	0	0	0	0
	H	1	0	0	0	0	0
	% of Mastery	100%	0%	0%	0%	0%	0%

Objectives

Key to coding: 0 — nonmastery
1 — mastery

When Wilson reviewed the data tables, he was very concerned. Only one student obtained mastery of the the terminal objective on the posttest! One hundred percent of the students achieved mastery of objective 1.0, but only 37.5 percent of the students attained mastery of objective 2.0. An acceptable 87 percent of the students achieved mastery of objective 3.0, but things went downhill from there. Seventy-five percent achieved

Figure 19.4   Students Mastering Objectives on Posttest

		Objectives					
		1.0	**2.0**	**3.0**	**4.0**	**5.0**	**6.0**
Students	A	1	1	1	1	0	0
	B	1	0	1	1	1	0
	C	1	1	1	0	1	0
	D	1	0	0	0	0	0
	E	1	0	1	1	1	0
	F	1	0	1	1	0	0
	G	1	1	1	1	1	1
	H	1	0	1	1	1	0
% of Mastery		100%	37.5%	87.0%	75.0%	62.5%	12.5%

Key to coding: 0 — nonmastery
1 — mastery

mastery of objective 4.0, 62.5 percent mastered objective 5.0, and only 12.5 percent mastered objective 6.0.

Things looked normal on the pretest. All the students seemed to possess the entry-level skills: at least they correctly answered the questions to which they responded. Objective 1.0 was mastered by every student on the pretest, but no additional questions were attempted, suggesting they lacked knowledge of the objectives the workbook was designed to teach. But based on the posttest results, the workbook wasn't very effective.

The students in the one-on-one evaluation didn't have that much trouble with the lesson. Wilson was determined to find out where the problem was. He had included practice items for most of the subskills in his instructional analysis, so perhaps an analysis of students' responses to those items could provide some clues as to where the problem was. He decided to look at the students' performance on embedded practice items for each objective (Figure 19.5).

When examining student performance on the practice items, Wilson found that 87 percent of the students were able to accomplish the tasks required by objective 2.0 as they worked through the workbook. In fact, the practice questions for each of the subskills leading to objective 2.0 were answered correctly by 87 percent or 100 percent of the students.

While completing the practice activities, 63 percent of the students achieved mastery on objective 3.0. Two of the subskills were achieved by 87 percent of the students, and 75 percent of them correctly answered all questions for objective 3.1. Wilson recalled that 87 percent of the students mastered objective 3.0 on the posttest.

Figure 19.5 Students Mastering Objectives on Practice Items

Practice Items

Objective	1.0	2.0	2.2.1.1	2.2.1	2.2	2.2.2.1	2.2.2.2	2.2.2	2.3.1	2.3	2.3.2.1	2.3.2.2	2.3.2.3	2.3.2	2.4	3.2	3.0	3.3
A	1	1	0	1	1	1	1	1	0	1	1	1	1	1	1	1	1	1
B	1	1	1	1	1	1	1	1	1	1	1	1	1	1	1	1	0	1
C	1	1	1	1	1	0	1	1	1	1	1	1	1	1	1	0	1	1
D	1	0	1	1	1	1	1	1	1	1	1	1	1	1	1	1	1	1
E	1	1	1	1	1	1	1	1	1	1	1	1	1	0	1	1	1	1
F	1	1	1	1	1	1	1	0	1	0	1	1	1	1	1	1	1	1
G	1	1	1	1	1	1	1	1	1	1	1	1	1	1	1	1	0	1
H	1	1	1	1	1	1	1	1	1	1	1	1	1	1	1	1	0	0
% mastery	100	87	87	100	100	87	100	87	87	87	100	100	100	87	100	87	63	87

Practice Items *Continued*

Objective	3.1	4.0	5.2.1	5.2.2	5.2	5.1	5.0	6.0
A	1	1	1	1	0	0	0	0
B	1	1	1	1	1	1	1	1
C	1	1	1	0	1	1	0	1
D	0	0	0	1	0	0	0	0
E	0	1	1	1	0	0	0	0
F	1	1	1	1	1	0	1	1
G	1	1	1	1	0	0	0	0
H	1	0	1	1	1	1	0	0
% mastery	75	75	87	87	50	38	25	38

Key to coding: 0 — less than 100% of questions correct for that objective
1 — 100% of questions correct for that objective

During the practice activities, objective 4.0 was achieved by 75 percent of the students. These results are consistent with their posttest performance.

Although an acceptable 87 percent of the students achieved mastery on the verbal information questions for subskills 5.2.1 and 5.2.2, only 25 percent of them achieved mastery on the performance-based question for objective 5.0. Wilson was surprised to see that more students mastered this objective on the posttest than within the context of the instructional workbook.

After he saw how poorly students had done on practice items for objective 5.0, he was not surprised that only 38 percent of the students achieved mastery on practice items for objective 6.0.

Wilson was confused. He sensed that there was some problem in the instruction but wasn't sure where it was. He decided to look at the student questionnaire for clues (Figure 19.6).

Figure 19.6   Results of Student Questionnaire

---

1.   **How difficult was the lesson?**
     0 - Too easy   8 - About right   0 - Too difficult
     Comments: All in one sitting was too much; hard, but I'm a beginner.

2.   **How was the vocabulary in the lesson?**
     0 - Too easy   8 - About right   0 - Too difficult
     Comments: None.

3.   **How was the length of the lesson?**
     8 - Too long   0 - About right   0 - Too short
     Comments: Don't give at night; students will get turned off.

4.   **How were the directions?**
     1 - Confusing   0 - Neutral   7 - Clear
     Comments: Sometimes confusing.

5.   **Would you like to use Logo?**
     2 - No   3 - Don't know   3 - Yes
     Comments: None.

6.   **How was the <u>number</u> of practice exercises?**
     0 - Too few   7 - About right   1 - Too many
     Comments: None.

7.   **How was the <u>wording</u> of the practice exercises?**
     0 - Confusing   3 - Neutral   5 - Clear
     Comments: Good feedback.

8.   **How did you like the illustrations in the lesson?**
     0 - Wasn't needed   1 - Neutral   7 - Helped me
     Comments: None.

Figure 19.6 *Continued*

9. **Did the posttest questions match the things taught in the unit?**
   0 - No   0 - Some did, some didn't   8 - Yes
   Comments: Very good.

10. **How were the test questions?**
    0 - Too easy   8 - About right   0 - Too difficult
    Comments: I'm slow.

11. **How was the <u>wording</u> of the test questions?**
    0 - Confusing   1 - Neutral   7 - Clear
    Comments: Need to know way turtle is facing.

12. **What did you think about the <u>number </u>of examples given in the lesson?**
    0 - Not enough   8 - About right   0 - Too many
    Comments: None.

13. **What did you think about the explanation of the illustrations that were given as examples?**
    0 - Confusing   1 - Neutral   7 - Clear
    Comments: None.

14. **How was the arrangement of instruction of the page?**
    0 - Too much   6 - About right   2 - Too crowded
     blank space
    Comments: None.

The questionnaire supported the verbal feedback received at the end of the small-group session. All the students felt that the lesson was too long. The rest of the feedback on the questionnaire was more positive. The majority of the students felt that the vocabulary level, difficulty level, number of practice exercises, test questions, number of examples, and arrangement of the instruction on the page were about right. The students responded that the directions, wording of test questions, and explanations of the instructions were clear. All students felt that the posttest questions matched the objectives taught in the lesson.

Wilson decided to look for possible patterns in the students' failure to master objectives at the criterion level established. He mapped their pretest and posttest scores onto the Instructional Analysis chart to look for clues (Figure 19.7). As he looked at all of his data, he began to see some patterns emerging.

Figure 19.7 Summary of Pretest and Posttest Scores for each Objective in Instructural Analysis

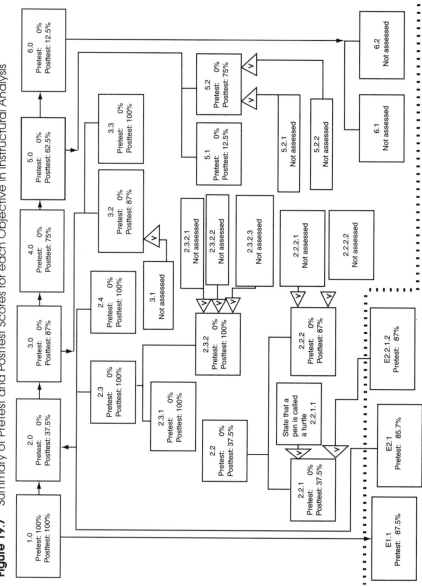

Invoking ID practice via the Roger Wilson case

1. Examine data to determine learners' initial skill level.
2. Analyze pretest and posttest data to determine learning gains (if any).
3. Examine evaluation data to identify problems with test items, student performance, or content delivery.
4. Examine evaluation data to identify design areas needing revision.

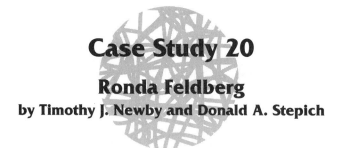

Case Study 20

Ronda Feldberg
by Timothy J. Newby and Donald A. Stepich

Ronda Feldberg sat in her office and reviewed the memo that had just arrived. It came from Barry Donovan, Vice President of Human Resources at McGraw International. As expected, he was requesting additional information on the development plans for her new training program. Within the memo, Donovan had set a meeting time in which Feldberg was to present a progress report and answer several key questions about the project. Other principal stakeholders would also be present. Feldberg knew she would need some time to gather information and prepare for her response/presentation.

She had been the manager of Corporate Training and Development at McGraw for a little less than a year. However, she had worked for McGraw for six years, the past three in the training and development department. McGraw is a large international corporation that manufactures and assembles engines for major automakers. They currently operate four production and assembly plants in the United States, two in Mexico, two in Europe, and one in Southeast Asia. A majority of their U.S.-produced engines are used in pickup trucks and sports utility vehicles. McGraw has earned a reputation for delivering an advanced reliable product, which has resulted in strong growth for the company. A major factor in maintaining McGraw's competitive edge has been its strong, proactive training department.

Because of frequent changes in engine design and manufacturing methods, McGraw has always done extensive technical training for both managers and line workers. Over the last year or so, the company has gradually shifted its management strategy to incorporate the use of work teams, especially in the manufacturing facilities. One result has been the development of a number of training courses aimed at increasing interpersonal skills in addition to their necessary focus on technical skills. Feldberg's current project is a course on "Interpersonal Communications." Donovan has seemed particularly interested in the development of the course and requested continual updates during the initial front-end analyses. During the last meeting Feldberg had mentioned the need to obtain information from potential participants to ensure the quality of the course. She saw this as a natural part of developing the course and had mentioned it almost as

an afterthought. However, Donovan questioned the need for this information, especially given the time and expense that would be involved in getting it. He wanted more information before making further funding
decisions pertaining to the course. His memo asked Feldberg to present
that information during a meeting scheduled for the following week.

After reflecting on the questions posed by Donovan in his memo,
Feldberg thought that she could probably use some advice from Jon
Giannopoulos. She had worked with him on previous training projects, and
he had more experience with evaluation than she did. Feldberg hoped
that he could provide some insights into her particular situation.
Giannopoulos had recently accepted a new assignment in the European
division and was now developing training courses at the Brussels office.
Feldberg sent an e-mail message, hoping that Giannopoulos would
respond in the next day or two. Her message read:

```
Message-ID:<m0wvoxC-000LKIC@macgraw>
Date: 20 Nov 1997
To: jgiannopoulos@mcgraweng.com
From: rfeldberg@mcgraweng.com

Hi Jon,

I hope all is going well for you in your new location. Living
out of a suitcase for several months is not my idea of fun,
but hopefully you are enjoying the assignment and you are
taking time to view the landscape.

I could really use some help. I've been working on a new
"Interpersonal Communications" (IC) course that will eventually
be added to the development curriculum for all employees.
We're still at the initial planning stage. Most of the
front-end analyses have been completed and we have established
the objectives for the course. Barry Donovan is the course
"champion" and he has stayed up to date as we've worked on
the course. Things have moved along smoothly until I suggest-
ed doing a thorough formative evaluation, which would
include obtaining information from participants to determine
how well they learned the material. Donovan has raised ques-
tions about this part of the project plan, most recently in
a memo to me. You know more about evaluation than I do so I
hoped I could "pick your brain" a bit.

As background, here are the course objectives that we have
identified to this point:

Following this course employees will be able to:

• Identify and describe differences in interpersonal commu-
nication styles
```

- Adapt their personal communication style in response to a given situation to improve working relationships

- Develop a strategy for effective communication with individuals, team members, and customers

- Demonstrate skills that effectively deal with tension that occurs in interpersonal interactions

- Improve team performance and individual relationships through reduced tension and more effective communication

- Develop a set of behaviors that promote trust in the workplace

Donovan didn't have any concerns about the objectives but has raised questions about the formative evaluation that I'd like to do. He's asked how the evaluation will occur—what procedures, types of evaluation instruments will be used, etc. More important, he's raised two "sticky" questions:

1. How will we convince upper management to provide the time and funding required for the suggested formative evaluation? Management's interest will be in rolling the course out as soon as possible.

2. How will we convince line personnel to be "tested" as part of the formative evaluation? Employees may think that their test performance will affect their performance reviews.

Donovan has a management meeting early next month. This course is on the agenda and he's asked me to help him present the project plan, particularly the formative evaluation component. He thinks that we may not get much support for the formative evaluation unless we can justify it in clear and convincing terms.

I have some ideas, but I would love to hear what you think would be the best course of action in terms of how it might be presented to management. Thanks a ton for your help.

Ronda

A day later, Feldberg received the following e-mail response:

Message-ID:<m0wvoxC-000TIMN@macgraweurope>
Date: 22 Nov 1997
To: rfeldberg@mcgraweng.com
From: jgiannopoulos@mcgraweng.com

Ronda —

We're doing well here. Busy, but things are going pretty well so far. We have spent some time taking in the sights

and Brussels is beautiful. Angela especially likes the
ceramics that are available here.

Sounds like you have your hands full with the IC course. I
know you asked for my advice, but I have more questions than
answers. Obviously, you know the details of the project better
than I do, but I have the advantage of distance, so maybe my
questions will help clarify some of the issues. Your e-mail
hints at two basic things to be concerned with: the plan and
the presentation.

First, the plan. Don't get too carried away. A thorough formative evaluation makes sense to me, but convincing me is
preaching to the choir. Think through the details of your
plan again. Management concerns with development schedules and
rollout dates are legitimate. So are employees' concerns about
being "tested." I think the question here is: How can you
make sure that the formative evaluation is as EFFICIENT as
possible? You'll have trouble justifying your plan if it
appears repetitive or wasteful in some way.

The other issue with the plan involves keeping people in the
loop. You've apparently done a good job communicating with
Donovan. Now, as the project progresses, think about who
else should be in the loop, why they should be there, and
what you can do to keep them there.

I think the presentation is a real opportunity. Remember how
we used to talk about the need to assert our value to the
organization? Here's your chance to educate people throughout the company about what we do, how we do it, and why we
do it that way. Here are some questions that occurred to me.
If you've already considered these issues, let me know.

Who will you be talking to? Management is the obvious
answer, since this is a management meeting. But who else in
the company will be concerned about your formative evaluation
plan? What questions and issues are they likely to have? How
might you respond to those questions and issues?

What do those people already know about formative evaluation? What preconceptions do they have? The antievaluation
forces may fall into one of three groups: those that don't
know anything about formative evaluation, those that don't
see how it applies to training, and those that don't believe
in its value for some reason.

You know as well as I do that management often agrees that
evaluation is important, but when the budgets are decided
they traditionally leave us with little time or money to do
the kind of evaluation we want.

What do you want them to know about formative evaluation
and how can you help them understand? Can you come up with

something that they already know about as a way of explaining the formative evaluation process and its importance? Product development, maybe. Everyone should know at least something about product development. Maybe you can use it to help them understand formative evaluation.

Finally, don't overwhelm them during your presentation, but give them specifics. They need to see that you've considered the problem from their perspectives, as well as from the training angle, and that you've thought through the details.

I've rambled enough. I hope this helps. I know your time is short, but let me know if you want to do some more brainstorming as you pull your plan and presentation together. By the way, when you get this figured out, let the rest of us know. Post your ideas on the training bulletin board as a way of sharing your success. This kind of problem comes up all the time, and anything you find that works will be a big help to the rest of us.

Good luck. Give my best to Jerry and say hi to the folks in the home office. .... Jon

Invoking ID practice via the Ronda Feldberg case

▶ Identify the stakeholders likely to be present at the meeting when Feldberg makes her presentation. Specify issues, concerns, and questions they may have about conducting a formative evaluation.

▶ Describe possible responses to each of the concerns listed earlier.

▶ Develop an analogy that Feldberg's audience might understand related to the value of and process for completing a formative evaluation.

▶ Develop a plan (and a rationale) for Feldberg's formative evaluation, including:
  ▶ Who will be involved
  ▶ How long it will take
  ▶ Procedures for gathering relevant data
  ▶ Procedures for analyzing data

▶ Discuss procedures for informing participants of their role in a formative evaluation.

▶ Develop a formative evaluation instrument that could be used to gather information about participants':
  ▶ knowledge/skills
  ▶ application of knowledge/skills

▶ Compare an "ideal" plan (no time or money constraints) with a "bare-bones" plan.

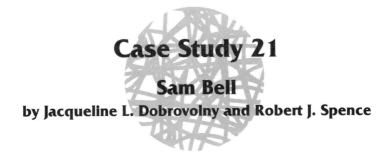

Case Study 21

Sam Bell

by Jacqueline L. Dobrovolny and Robert J. Spence

Sam Bell sat in his office staring out the window and enjoying the calmness of the early morning. He came in early since he didn't sleep well last night. He kept reflecting on the discussion he had yesterday during lunch with his long-time friend, David Townsend, a marketing executive with a local manufacturing company. Bell received some advice from Townsend that seemed simple enough, but he just wasn't sure it would work. As he drank his coffee, he reviewed the chain of events leading up to his current dilemma.

As the training manager for NorthCentral Bank (NCB), Bell was responsible for implementing a new computer-based training (CBT) curriculum in 2000 branch offices, which employ 37,000 people. He was very conscious of the responsibility and keen to make a success of what all the officers of the bank saw as a significant project. If he were successful, it probably meant a promotion and significant raise. If the CBT project were not successful, he figured he would have to look for a new job. The stakes were high.

Bell recalled two significant events that precipitated this whole situation. First, over the last 18 months, the competition had increased significantly. As a result, the bank needed to reduce costs and to operate as efficiently as possible. Second, NCB had always emphasized on-the-job training within each branch. In some cases, this training had been supplemented with group-paced courses at centralized locations. Three years ago, NCB began replacing the group-paced courses with paper-based, self-paced instructional materials, which were designed to teach specific, procedural issues and teller skills.

Bell was in charge of all of this training and found that the amount of maintenance required for the paper-based materials was tremendous. It was time consuming and costly because thousands of pieces of paper had to be updated annually. Competitor pressures, the need to reduce costs, together with the expense of maintenance, helped convince Bell that CBT was an attractive solution. Along with the accounting department, he performed numerous cost-benefit analyses, which demonstrated how CBT would reduce costs significantly. Bell and two of his trainers also conducted an extensive evaluation of the major CBT authoring systems. They purchased the system that rated highest in their evaluation. They also purchased a compatible graphics development package.

Bell selected 12 developers from NCB's training department. All of them volunteered for this project and all were subject-matter experts—that is, all began their career as tellers with NCB. The CBT development team currently consists of two instructional designers, four writers/subject-matter experts, two graphic artists, two authoring systems programmers, one editor, one evaluation expert, and Bell, the project manager. The graphic artists have received training on the use of the graphics software, and the authoring systems programmers have received training on the use of the authoring system.

The CBT development team established standards and procedures for courseware production. They decided to deliver the courseware via CD-ROM and PCs connected to NCB's proprietary intranet.

The teller training course is currently under development. Assuming no major problems, it should be ready for beta test in approximately six months. The beta test is scheduled to take three months, and revisions—on the basis of the beta test—are scheduled to take two months. Thus, the teller training course will be delivered to the 2000 branches in approximately 11 months.

The development of the CBT teller course has been great fun for the development team. Everyone on the team is excited about the project and confident that trainees will receive it enthusiastically. Everyone who sees the CBT has been impressed with the quality of the graphics, animations, and video clips.

Early last week, Bell visited some branch offices to select those that would participate in beta testing. To his surprise, rather than encountering enthusiasm from the training supervisors at the various branches, the mood was, at best, skeptical. Even Jane Harris, a friend of his who is well known and whose opinions are respected, was cautious. Her parting comment when Bell left her office was, "Sam, I really am concerned that we aren't ready for this technology stuff."

On the flight home that day Bell felt like someone had let all the air out of his balloon. He pondered Harris' comments. He was mystified and could not understand why she and the other training supervisors didn't share his enthusiasm for the CBT. The more he thought about it, the more panic he could feel rising up from his gut. He believed the skepticism of the training supervisors could lead to the rejection of the CBT teller training.

The day after that trip, Bell began searching for anything he could find on the introduction of new technology, resistance to change, and implementation problems specific to the use of technology. His reading led him to believe that the training supervisors were likely to resist CBT because of the following:

1. Most of the training supervisors took teller training at a centralized location in a group-paced format. Those who took the self-paced, paper-based training were generally not happy with that format.

2. The training supervisors have little experience with PCs other than through their banking work, which is done via PCs connected to a local-area network within each branch. When there is a problem with the banking software, the training supervisors turn it over to a software expert. If there is a problem with the CBT, the training supervisors will have to solve the problem themselves.

3. The teller training course contains an extensive computer-managed instructional (CMI) component that will track trainee performance. Training supervisors will be required to review that data to determine how individual trainees are performing and to periodically upload that data from the local server to the evaluation server.

4. There is no funding for an installation team to visit each branch and set up the teller training. Nor is there any funding to send the training supervisors to a group-paced course. Thus, each branch will receive a new PC that contains the teller training course and each branch will "self-install" their own system using documentation that will come with the PC.

These insights were heartbreaking! Bell could see his career at NCB coming to a quick and disappointing end.

Early this week, he received a call from Townsend, who wanted to meet him for lunch to catch up on all that had happened since they had seen each other almost six months ago. At first, Bell declined, explaining he was just too busy and had too many crises to handle. However, Townsend persisted, so they met yesterday at a restaurant close to Bell's office.

During lunch, Bell described his situation and his fears and concerns about the resistance to CBT. Townsend listened attentively but at first had no suggestions. As the waiter cleared their table, Townsend suddenly frowned and then looking Bell straight in the eye, said "This is a marketing problem, Sam! You are introducing a new product and you have to convince your users to buy it."

Invoking ID practice via the Sam Bell case

1. Stakeholders are those who have a personal interest or "stake" in something. Who are the stakeholders in this case? Describe their roles and importance in this case.

2. Who are the change agents in this case? Describe their roles and importance in this case.

3. Identify the decision to implement CBT at NCB as either a top-down or bottom-up decision. Provide examples or a rationale for your choice. Given the type of decision exemplified in this case, how do you think the training supervisors might take ownership of the CBT? What strategy or set of strategies might facilitate ownership?

4. The five stages people typically go through (adapted from Dormant, 1992, pp. 179–180) in adopting a new idea or new technology are:
    ▶ Awareness
    ▶ Self-concern or curiosity
    ▶ Visualization or mental tryout
    ▶ Hands-on trial and learning
    ▶ Adoption and use

    In what stage is Bell? In what stage is Harris? Provide support or examples for your choices.

5. Describe strategies for gaining support from stakeholders when implementing a new approach to training.

REFERENCES

Dormant, D. (1992). Implementing human performance technology in organizations. In H.D. Stolovitch, and E.J. Keeps (Eds.), *Handbook of human performance technology: A comprehensive guide for analyzing and solving performance problems in organizations* (pp. 167–187). San Francisco: Jossey-Bass.

Case Study 22

Sam Gonzales
by Brenda Sugrue

Atlantic Airlines was expanding and was about to hire 200 new flight attendants. The existing corps of flight attendants had been working with the airline for an average of five years and, based on current evaluations (customer satisfaction and supervisor ratings), was doing a very good job. The director of Human Performance Technology, Sam Gonzales, wanted to increase the consistency between the criteria used to evaluate performance at the end of training and criteria for judging on-the-job performance.

He decided that asking trainees to answer questions about video-taped situations would increase the authenticity of end-of-training assessments. He planned to try out his idea with one group of twenty trainees for two of the eighteen performance goals included in the basic training. He selected the goals of "performing preflight checks" and "dealing with difficult passengers" from the job map of level 1 flight attendants (Figure 22.1). For each goal, he asked his instructional designer, Linda McMillan, to:

1. Write a performance goal to represent each task in the job map;
2. For each of the eight situations, make a short video recording of an experienced flight attendant performing the task correctly, and two video recordings of the same flight attendant making two different commonly made errors in the situation.

Thus, sixteen video clips, each lasting about two minutes, were produced. Half of the clips were to be used as practice activities during the training, and half were to be used as end-of-training assessments. The end-of-training clips were embedded in a computer program that asked students related questions.

Sam thought that ability to identify errors in the performance of the attendants in the video clips would predict ability to actually perform well in situations similar to those portrayed in the videos. He was convinced that this type of assessment would be more valid than the previous end-of-training assessments that were paper-and-pencil tests. The paper-and-pencil tests had a variety of types of questions, including multiple-choice questions that asked trainees to select the correct sequence of steps for

Figure 22.1 Simplified job map for level 1 flight attendants

Atlantic Airlines Flight Attendant Level 1 Job Map

Safety — Preflight / During flight | demos checks
Emergencies — Landings / Evacuations / First aid

Service — Beverage / Food
First Class | Coach Class
National | International
Children and passengers with special needs

Communication — Using PC systems / Routine requests / Difficult passengers

performing various tasks, and questions that depicted situations and asked students to write short answers describing what should be done in the situation.

Gonzales also thought that short-answer items were too time consuming to score and that the new "multimedia" assessments should have only multiple-choice questions, administered by computers to permit automatic scoring and immediate generation of data. The items related to a video clip would typically ask students to (1) identify what job task was being performed in the video, from a list of choices, (2) decide if the attendant in the video made any errors in performing the task, and (3) if there were errors, identify what they were, from a list of choices, or (4) if there were no errors, identify the most critical aspect of the attendant's performance in the video, from a list of choices. Scores for any one video scenario could range from 0 to 8. An example of the questions that accompanied one "difficult passenger" video is provided in Figure 22.2.

Once selected, the trainees completed their training in groups of twenty, each with a different instructor, with one group of twenty using the new assessments (instead of pencil-and-paper tests) on the two selected performance goals (preflight checks and dealing with difficult passengers). This group received the same assessments as every other group on all other performance goals. Some of the trainees in this group were concerned about how the new assessments would affect their overall end-of-training scores, but they were not allowed to switch to another group. When the end-of-training results came out, the overall results of this group were slightly lower than the other groups. Two students (students 1 and 17 in Table 22.1) who got particularly low scores were upset and blamed their low scores on the new assessments. They wrote a letter to Gonzales stating that the new assessments were unfair and that they should be allowed to complete the

Figure 22.2 Sample multiple-choice questions to accompany a video clip

1. Which of the following job tasks is illustrated in the video?
   a. Serving dinner on an international flight.
   b. Responding to a common passenger request.
   c. Dealing with a difficult passenger.
   d. Dealing with a passenger with special needs.

2. Did the attendant in the video make any errors?
   a. Yes.
   b. No.
   c. I'm not sure.
      If yes, question 3 would be displayed.
      If no, question 4 would be displayed.
      If not sure, question 5 would be displayed.

3. Which of the following errors did the attendant make?
   a. She did not ask the passenger to come to the back of the cabin so that she could discuss the problem.
   b. She did not smile.
   c. She did not promise the passenger that she would mention the problem to the supervisor.
   d. She did not repeat the passenger's concern in her own words.
   e. a. and b.
   f. b. and d.

4. Which of the following actions was the most critical aspect of the attendant's behavior in this situation?
   a. She isolated the passenger from other passengers.
   b. She talked to her supervisor.
   c. She repeated the passenger's concern back to him.
   d. She did not appear annoyed.
   e. a. and c.
   f. b. and c.

5. Which of the following makes you unsure?
   a. The situation appeared to be resolved.
   b. You did not spend enough time studying this aspect of the course.
   c. The attendant in the video did not follow the procedure you learned exactly and that confused you.
   d. The situation did not appear to be resolved.

old set of questions for the two performance goals that had brought their overall scores down. The instructor who taught the special group also complained that the new assessments were more difficult than the paper-and-pencil tests for those performance goals, and that the new assessments made it look as if he were not a good instructor. He suggested to Gonzales that the multimedia assessments be abandoned.

Figure 22.3 Checklist for evaluating performance when dealing with a difficult passenger

1. Did the attendant listen carefully to the passenger's complaint?	____
2. Did the attendant paraphrase the passenger's complaint back to him/her?	____
3. Did the attendant offer the passenger the simplest solution to the problem first?	____
4. Was the attendant polite during the entire interaction?	____
5. Did the attendant maintain a normal tone of voice during the entire interaction?	____
6. Was the passenger reassured and calm by the end of the interaction?	____
Total points (out of 6)	____

To make an informed decision, Gonzales asked for a complete breakdown of the data for the twenty students on the multimedia assessments. He also asked for the on-the-job evaluation data for this group of students on tasks related to the performance goals measured by the new assessments. During the first two months after training, the performance of trainees was evaluated on the job. Scores on each on-the-job task evaluation could range from 0 to 6. The checklist used to evaluate performance in dealing with difficult passengers is shown in Figure 22.3.

You are a consultant hired to help Gonzales interpret the data and come to a decision regarding the future of the new assessments.

▶ Relevant Data

Table 22.1 shows scores for all twenty students on end-of-training assessments for the two performance goals. Figure 22.4 shows average performance across the eight end-of-training video assessments. The traditional measure of reliability (Cronbach's alpha) was .49 if one considered the four end-of-training scores as a single measure of mastery of performance goal 1. If one considered the four video clips as measuring two different aspects of performance—ability to handle routine tasks and ability to deal with unusual situations related to that goal—the reliability coefficients increased to .72 and .75 for frequent and unusual situations, respectively. Cronbach's alpha for performance goal 2 (considering the four clips as measuring the same goal) was .32; when frequent and unusual situations are treated as separate subgoals, coefficients increased to .40 and .61, indicating that the two frequently occurring clips for performance goal 2 were not yielding comparable estimates for some students.

Figure 22.5 shows the performance of the two students (students 1 and 17) who complained that the assessments were unfair. Table 22.2 shows total end-of-training scores for the two performance goals and average performance in a situation on the job that corresponded to each goal. The correlation between end-of-training and on-the-job performance scores was .95. Typically, correlation between end-of-training pencil-and-paper assessments and on-the-job evaluations was .80.

Table 22.1 Scores on end-of-training video assessments for two performance goals

Trainee	Performance Goal 1 Preflight checks				Performance Goal 2 Dealing with difficult passengers			
	Frequent Situations		Unusual Situations		Frequent Situations		Unusual Situations	
	Clip 1	Clip 2	Clip 3	Clip 4	Clip 5	Clip 6	Clip 7	Clip 8
1	4	4	6	2	2	4	6	4
2	8	8	6	4	6	8	6	6
3	8	8	2	0	8	6	4	2
4	8	4	4	4	8	8	4	4
5	2	4	4	2	4	6	6	6
6	8	8	2	0	8	6	4	2
7	6	6	6	2	8	6	6	4
8	8	8	8	4	8	8	6	6
9	6	8	4	0	8	4	4	2
10	6	6	6	4	8	6	6	0
11	6	6	8	2	6	6	6	4
12	8	8	2	0	8	6	4	2
13	4	4	6	2	4	6	6	6
14	8	8	6	6	6	8	6	6
15	8	8	4	0	8	8	6	2
16	6	6	8	4	8	8	4	4
17	2	4	4	2	2	6	3	2
18	8	2	6	0	8	6	4	2
19	8	6	6	6	8	6	8	8
20	8	8	8	4	6	8	8	2
Mean	6.5	6.2	5.3	2.4	6.6	6.5	5.35	3.7

Figure 22.4   Average performance on end-of-training video assessments

Average Performance Across Video Clips

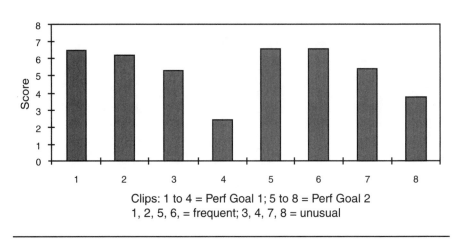

Clips: 1 to 4 = Perf Goal 1; 5 to 8 = Perf Goal 2
1, 2, 5, 6, = frequent; 3, 4, 7, 8 = unusual

Figure 22.5   Profile of scores of two low-scoring students on end-of-training assessments

Student 1 and 17: End-of-Training Scores

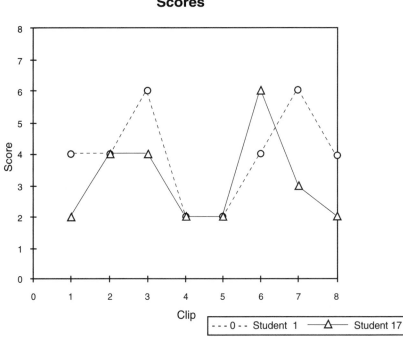

Table 22.2   Total scores on end-of-training and on-the-job performance for two performance goals

| Trainee | Performance Goal 1 Preflight Safety Checks | | Performance Goal 2 Dealing with Difficult Passengers | |
	End of Training (max = 32)	On the Job (max = 6)	End of Training (max = 32)	On the Job (max = 6)
1	16	3	16	3
2	26	6	26	6
3	18	4	20	4
4	20	4	24	5
5	12	2	22	5
6	18	4	20	4
7	20	4	24	5
8	28	6	28	6
9	18	4	18	4
10	22	5	20	4
11	22	5	22	5
12	18	4	20	4
13	16	3	22	5
14	28	6	26	6
15	20	4	24	5
16	24	5	24	5
17	12	2	13	2
18	16	3	20	4
19	26	6	30	6
20	28	6	24	6
Mean	20.4	4.3	22.15	4.7

Correlation between end-of-training and on-the-job performance = .95

Invoking ID practice via the Sam Gonzales case

1. Distinguish between the various purposes of assessment in instructional design.
2. Determine the reliability and validity of the assessment instruments in this case.
3. Analyze data to determine weaknesses in instruction.
4. Analyze data to diagnose students' performances.
5. Compare the usefulness of data gathered on the job to data gathered after training as the basis for making instructional decisions.

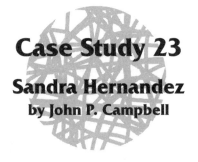

Case Study 23

Sandra Hernandez
by John P. Campbell

Sandra Hernandez was a new faculty member in the College of Engineering who arrived at the college touted as a "super teacher." She won numerous teaching awards as a graduate student and had just started her first position as an assistant professor. Previously she was an aerospace engineer for nearly 10 years. Her first teaching assignment was the "Engineering Methods and Graphical Communications" course required by all freshmen. Hernandez soon discovered that this assignment was not a "prize" assignment, but one that other faculty did not want.

The "Engineering Methods and Graphical Communications" course is an introduction to engineering design, data collection, and visual representation. The goal of the course is to develop a strong conceptual understanding of basic engineering principles, including fluid dynamics, electricity, and force. Students practice developing hypotheses, setting up experiments, collecting data, and presenting results. Hernandez was frustrated with the lack of laboratory equipment, which was further complicated by the large number of students. During an average semester, there are 8 sections of 30 students. To help with the teaching load, Hernandez was assigned three graduate engineering students. Last semester, the first semester she coordinated, the class was a disaster. She felt she had not adequately covered the content and felt frustrated that the students did not have enough hands-on and real-world experiences.

During a typical class, students are given basic engineering problems. For example, a problem may look like this:

> If water from a bathroom sink (capacity 4 gallons, 18-inch diameter) is drained into a basin 2 feet below the sink using a standard 1-inch PVC pipe, what will the flow rate be? What happens if the sink basin is increased in diameter? What type of relationship exists? What happens to the flow rate if the drainpipe diameter is changed? What type of relationship exists?

The students are then required to set up the experiment and collect data. Often they are rushing to complete the experiment, forcing the next section to be late starting. Hernandez was convinced that the general goal of getting students to make informed predictions on basic engineering concepts is valid, but she needed to find new ways of approaching the class.

She decided to visit the Instructional Development Center (IDC) on campus even though she was worried about the time involved. The center was established to help faculty with a variety of instructional problems and consists of a staff of 14 professionals serving nearly 2000 faculty. The staff have a variety of backgrounds, including instructional designers, programmers, graphic artists, evaluation specialists, and publication designers. Hernandez's case was assigned to Jake Spaulding. Spaulding was an instructional designer who was hired six months previously. Although new to the center, he had spent the two previous years as a designer for a major consulting company. He came to the university to complete his doctoral degree and found it difficult learning to deal with this new type of client. He often found that faculty priorities were more focused on research than teaching. He mentioned that working with faculty was as difficult as "herding cats."

Spaulding met Hernandez in her office on the other side of campus. "So, Professor Hernandez, how can the Instructional Development Center help you?"

Hernandez responded, "First, please call me Sandra. I have never adjusted to being called professor. I don't have much time, so let me give you a quick synopsis. I am currently in charge of the 'Engineering Methods and Graphical Communications' course. The course is designed to provide students with hands-on experiences revolving around various engineering principles. Few incoming college students have a strong conceptual understanding of the basic principles such as fluid dynamics, electricity, and force. Their lack of conceptual understanding, whether attributed to poor academic preparation or few hands-on experiences, has a profound impact on future engineering courses. Students have difficulty in the laboratory distinguishing correct answers from those answers that are 'unlikely' or 'way off.' Additionally, they have trouble applying what is learned in the classroom to producing engineering design solutions."

"So where do problems occur?" Spaulding asked.

Hernandez explained the difficulty in providing students with realistic examples. She continued by describing how students often spend two or more hours of a three-hour lab just setting up one portion of the lab. Students often "waste" time during the setup and fail to collect enough data. "I like using a hands-on approach, but there has to be a more effective use of class time. The problems get even more complicated when you consider a topic such as fluid dynamics. Students are conducting experiments with plastic tubing and PVC pipe but are unable to 'envision' other factors of fluid dynamics."

She continued, "Students need to develop hypotheses concerning the physical relationships between various elements of a fluid system, construct a simulated system, collect data, and evaluate their results. The ultimate pedagogical goal is to help students develop a better conceptual understanding of these relationships within fluid systems. I believe that if they are going to achieve this goal, they need to be able to experiment with more elements of fluid systems. It would be especially valuable if they could use different types and sizes of pipes and fluids. But I'm getting carried away; the time and budget do not even begin to allow them to reach that goal."

"As an instructor, is the fluid dynamics portion of the course one of the most difficult parts to teach?" Spaulding asked.

Hernandez thought the fluid dynamics portion was a good place to start, so they agreed to meet again. In this meeting, Spaulding asked Hernandez to describe the ideal fluid dynamics lab. Below is his summary of key elements:

▸ Provide students with a variety of real-world lab experiments

▸ Allow use of a variety of pipe components, including 90° elbows, 45° elbows, and different-sized tanks

▸ Allow the addition of flow valves and meters at any point in the system to collect data

▸ Allow placement of a pressure gauge at any point in the system

▸ Allow use of a variety of pipe materials and sizes, particularly concrete, copper, PVC, and steel

▸ Provide use of a variety of fluids, including crude oil, kerosene, molasses, and water

Hernandez was frustrated by the end of the conversation. She did not see how describing her view of an ideal fluid lab would help her when resources and time were limited. Before leaving the meeting, however, she provided Spaulding with three additional problems she would like students to solve.

1. Show that if a typical bathroom sink (capacity 4 gallons, 18-inch diameter) is drained into a basin 2 feet below the sink using a standard 1-inch PVC pipe, the flow rate will be from 7.2 to 6.7 feet per second. How long does it take for a full sink to empty?

2. A pump is required to move water from a large reservoir to a point 120 feet above the base of the reservoir. The pump head is 155 feet. If the volumetric flow rate is to be approximately 125 gallons per minute, when there is 3 feet of water in the reservoir, select the pipe from those available: (a) 150 feet of 3-inch PVC, (b) 130 feet of 2-inch PVC, (c) 125 feet of 3-inch steel, or (d) 130 feet of 2-inch copper.

3. A small pump is to be used to pump water from the reservoir tank to the filter holder in a new design of a coffee maker. Assume you have 0.25 gallon of water to transport. Knowing that the system (tubing, pump, and reservoir) must fit within in a 4-inch-wide, 8-inch-high, and 4-inch-deep volume, lay out the design so that you can achieve a "quick" pot of coffee. Note: The 4-inch by 4-inch by 8-inch space does not include space for filter or pot.

Justify your design by describing: (1) the relative cost, (2) feasibility, and (3) practicality. Spaulding was becoming more and more puzzled. Not understanding fluid dynamics, he attempted to gather more information from Hernandez via e-mail. During their exchange, he was able to collect information about her ideal instructional capabilities. His summary of the information is shown in the Table 23.1.

Invoking ID practice via the Sandra Hernandez case

1. What problems did Hernandez present in this case?
2. What additional data are needed to get a better picture of the problems? How would you collect the necessary data?
3. Suggest possible solutions to the presenting problems, taking into account the resource requirements and potential constraints for various solutions.
4. Suggest implementation strategies for the solutions described in question 3.

Table 23.1 Ideal Lab Capabilities

Element	Options
Pipe	Materials: steel, concrete, PVC, and copper Length: inches to 10,000 feet Diameter: 0.125 to 84 inches
Fluid Types	Water, oil, molasses, kerosene
Connections	45° and 90° elbows
Valves	Ability to set valve at 0%, 25%, 50%, 75%, and 100% open
Pump	Pump head specified by user in feet or pounds per square inch (psi)
Tanks	Inlet and outlets on top and bottom of tanks. Capacity ranging from cubic inches to infinite reservoirs
Data Collection	Pressure gauge Flow meters Temperature gauge Time clock

Case Study 24

Terry Kirkland

by M. Elizabeth Hrabe, Valerie A. Larsen, and Mable B. Kinzie

"Needs analysis! Why should we want a needs analysis? We already know what we want to do!"

Five heads nodded in agreement as I looked around the table. I tried to read the expressions on the faces of the members of the Workplace Readiness Project Committee: irritation? speculation? boredom? hostility? This was my first meeting with the committee and my hopes for it going well were rapidly collapsing.

I had been hired as an instructional designer exactly one week before by Dr. Jim Cranston, the new Assistant Superintendent for Instruction and Vocational services. The Dundee County school system had obtained a small grant for the development of a series of workshops that would introduce high school students to the workplace readiness skills most desired by employers. The workshops were intended to serve as a pilot project for later implementation in all three of the county high schools. The project had been "in committee" for a year and had never gotten off the ground, and the school board had made the decision to bring in an instructional designer to structure the plan and ensure its successful execution. Although this was only my second job as an instructional designer, Dr. Cranston seemed to like my ideas. "You haven't had any experience working with teachers," he cautioned toward the end of our interview, "so it will be important that you take command right away. I know you can do it." His confidence in me and enthusiasm for the undertaking had been contagious. I left his office looking forward to working with this committee in creating an effective and dynamic design for instruction. Now I was not so sure.

I arrived at Dundee High School in the afternoon to attend this first project meeting and learned from Mavis Barrett, the assistant principal, that Dr. Cranston had called to say he'd be unable to attend. He was to have introduced me and explained my role to the other members of the committee.

Ms. Barrett had been pleasant enough, but appeared harried by the constant interruptions and distractions that constitute much of the job of a front-line administrator. We had little time for coherent conversation, although she did manage to give me a brief description of the teachers I would be working with in creating and implementing the project.

Jane Pruitt, lead teacher in the business department, had been highly involved with trying to get the project off the ground the year before. The rest of the committee tended to defer to her knowledge of the proposed workshop content, the authority that came naturally with a dominating personality and her 25 years of experience in the trenches. Suzanne Fuentes, the English teacher, and Len Gold, social studies, were holdover members of the committee and supported the concept that all students would benefit from learning skills that would make them employable in the future. Finally, Dwight Harris, the technology education teacher, had been newly assigned to the committee this year. Although he and the others received a small stipend for the after-school work, he had been blunt in expressing his unhappiness at having been pressed into service.

When Ms. Barrett finally introduced me to the committee, I had the feeling that they were somewhat underwhelmed by my presence. They had only recently been told that an outside instructional designer was being brought in to design the workshops. Proving myself might be a little more difficult than I had anticipated.

Armed with the committee recommendations from the previous year, I had carefully prepared my presentation. I began by explaining that it would be necessary to begin the design process with a needs assessment. My announcement was greeted by a stony silence...which soon gave way to a litany of protests.

Jane Pruitt was vehement. "Look, Terry, didn't they tell you when they hired you? We decided on the content for our school to job workshop last year. We are going to teach students how to write résumés and fill out applications. I have done a unit that includes these skills in my 'Intro to Business' class every year and I know exactly how to do it."

Suzanne Fuentes added, "Also, I really don't think we have the time for such a thing. We're starting late as it is."

"Yeah," chimed in Dwight Harris. "What the hell is a 'needs analysis' anyway? Sounds like a bunch of jargon!" He did not say more, but I could feel him thinking, "Is that what they're paying you for? Fancy words?"

"Whoa! Folks! Calm down." Mavis Barrett invoked her role as committee chair. "Don't bite our designer's head off. Remember, we have a mandate from above. The powers downtown think this is important and they have sent us help. Let's use it."

BLEEP! BLEEP! The chirp of Mavis' ever-present beeper punctuated her observation. "Sorry, gotta go," she said, rising. She shot me an apologetic smile and then addressed the others, "Seriously, give Terry a chance to explain." And she was out the door.

As I reluctantly turned back to face the lions, Len Gold laughed. "Okay, Terry. Do your thing. We'll listen."

Grabbing the friendly invitation, I quickly explained the reasons for doing a needs analysis and the design process itself. As I warmed to my topic, the others seemed to be listening—with the exception of Jane, who sat leaning back from the table with arms folded across her chest.

Even when the others agreed to my conducting a needs assessment, Jane remained silent. She was not so passive when the meeting broke up, however. Speaking loudly to Dwight, she swept out of the room, "Maybe if they had given us the money they used to hire this Kirkland person, we could have gotten this project going last year!"

Two weeks later, immediately following the Thanksgiving holiday, the project committee reconvened.

" … and so I think that we should reconsider the objectives for the workshop instruction. It seems clear that résumés and employment applications, though clearly important, are not what potential employers indicate they most want to see in their new employees."

Surveying my fellow committee members, I wondered how they felt about the needs analysis I had just presented. I felt confident that my report was comprehensive and the information accurate. Even though the results conflicted with the expectations of the group, I sensed a surge of interest in my assertion that the employers I interviewed had expressed a desire to see students develop skills in conflict management, cooperation with others, and problem solving. They had also laid great stress on the importance of a good attendance record.

Both Suzanne and Len agreed that these were important attitudes and skills for all of the students to possess, even those in the most academic Advanced Placement track. Jane, however, remained adamant, insisting that first impressions were most critical and that it was well-done applications, résumés, and job interviews that would get them the jobs they wanted.

BLEEP! Once again Mavis was summoned from our midst.

"And there's another thing to consider, Terry," Jane continued, not missing a beat. "I know when my students can write good résumés and fill out applications properly. It's measurable. How can you measure such soft skills as 'cooperation' and 'managing conflict'?"

"Good point," I admitted. "Actually there are two things to be considered here. First, we have asked representatives of the business community what they consider most important. They have responded and, in good faith, we need to address their concerns—not substitute what we want simply because it is easier and more convenient for us. Besides, as it turns out, these are the same skills listed by employers in a national study commissioned by the Department of Labor." I showed them the latest SCANS report.[1] Recommendations included, in addition to basic academics, that students be prepared in critical thinking, problem solving, decision making, self-management, and accepting responsibility.

---

[1]The Secretary's Commission on Achieving Necessary Skills. (1991). *What work requires of schools: A SCANS report for America 2000.* Washington, DC: U.S. Department of Labor.

"And second, as far as evaluation is concerned," I continued hastily since Jane seemed to have shut down momentarily, "we don't have to use pencil-and-paper tests to find out if students have developed these abilities."

"I use observation check-off lists and team evaluations with my classes now," added Dwight, suddenly thoughtful. "Those work pretty well."

"Yes," Len jumped in. "We can devise activities that will allow us to observe students employing these skills in practice—role playing, group task completion, things like that. And then, perhaps, we teachers could have follow-up discussions and class projects that would show how well what they learned lasted over time."

For the next hour, we proceeded to hash out our major goals, objectives, and assessment possibilities in this manner. I could scarcely breathe when finally I asked, "Then, we're all agreed?" Everyone nodded in approval except Jane, whose impassive silence I decided to take for assent.

Our plans shaped up. We wanted to include all of the junior class in our workshop. Since there were approximately 180 students involved, we had to schedule the workshop to be repeated 4 times with about 45 students attending each session. We agreed that each workshop would last for 3 hours, with morning and afternoon sessions repeated over 2 consecutive days. The workshop dates were set for March 4–5 and a note was written for Mavis to add these activities to the school calendar.

I spent the next few days developing the schedule of tasks/responsibilities we would have to complete to meet the March deadline (Figure 24.1).

Since we had (nearly) unanimously agreed on the content and activities for our workshops, I went on to complete a design that incorporated our goals and objectives. Later Len called to tell me he had secured Don McKay as our facilitator. McKay, he assured me, had an outstanding reputation and was known to have a way with teenagers.

On February 18, I was summoned to an emergency meeting of the project committee. A severe winter storm had shut down the school system for the last week and that, together with several days missed in January, had really pushed back our work schedule on the Workshop project. However, it was the undertone of worry in Mavis Barrett's voice when she had called to schedule today's committee meeting that had set off a silent alarm bell in my head. What was the matter now?

As I rounded the corner of the corridor that led to the small conference room where the committee met, I could hear the murmur of conversation. I recognized Jane's voice rising discordantly above the others. "I'm telling you, she doesn't know what she's doing. I've heard that she's had only one other job before this. Listen, if you ask me, this is going to be a disaster and who will they blame? Little Miss Fix-it will be long gone. It's us, that's who!"

Figure 24.1 Committee Tasks/Assignments

Develop workshop activities	
Facilitator's guide	Terry, Suzanne, Len
Get resources, materials	Terry, Dwight
Design and produce program	Terry, Suzanne
Workshop Arrangements	
Arrange dates	Mavis
Arrange for room, equipment	Mavis, Dwight
Contact and train facilitator	Terry, Len
Contact guest speaker	Terry, Jane
Invite guests	Mavis, Suzanne
Evaluations	
Design formative evaluation	Terry
Set dates, arrange logistics	Jane
Arrange for facilitator (formative)	Jane
Select student sample	Jane
Carry out formative evaluation	Terry, Len, Suzanne
Write up results	Terry
Make changes	Committee
Design workshop evaluation	Terry
Conduct evaluation	Terry, Len, Suzanne, Jane, Dwight
Write up results	Terry

I hesitated before entering the room. I recognized how imperative it was to demonstrate some decisive leadership so that the committee would continue to believe in this project. I decided a positive attitude might help to counter Jane's negativity.

Everyone was there—except Mavis, who was closeted with an angry parent. Len waved hello and Dwight shouted, "Well, hello, Ms. Designer! Guess what? We've got a problem. Sorry, make that problems!"

Suzanne, who had been huddled over a paper with Jane, looked up and said, "Hi, Terry. I'm afraid Dwight's right about the problems." Her face betrayed worry and her greeting was tentative.

"Hey, guys," I said, assuming as bright a smile as I could muster, "we're the A-team here. There's no problem we can't handle!"

As it turned out, the first difficulty was easy enough to deal with. In spite of my memo, Mavis had scheduled activities that conflicted with our first workshop session. The school's calendar was jammed and the only other available time was an afternoon three days sooner. "Terry, are you sure we can do this?" asked Suzanne.

I was calm and reassuring. "Yes, of course. But we really have to get cracking."

The other problem was somewhat more complicated. Jane had not been able to round up a representative sample of students and a willing facilitator for the formative evaluation. "Oh, you know how kids are, they've always got too much to do! Besides, you've done such a superior job at designing your workshop, I'm sure it's just perfect. There's nothing to get all bent out of shape about."

I wanted to bend Jane out of shape . . . but I bit my tongue. She remained on the committee after her own plans for the workshops had been overruled, but her contributions were casual at best.

"Well, actually, we really do need a formative evaluation of our materials and procedures. We have to know what works and what does not," I addressed the rest of the group, ignoring Jane. "This is a really important project and a lot of people are invested in it. You all know that."

"I have an idea," offered Len. "My second-period history class would be a good test for the workshop."

"Oh, yeah. Your remedials!" This from Dwight.

"Not all of them. But, certainly, some are," Len continued, his enthusiasm beginning to grow. "These kids are a hard audience. You really have to sell them. If they don't like something, they are not polite about letting you know. They would give us a real shakedown cruise."

Dwight remained somewhat dubious, but Suzanne and Jane were warming to the idea. After all, with little more than a week before our first scheduled workshop, what else could we do?

It was, therefore, agreed to use Len's class for the formative evaluation with Len himself acting as facilitator.

The formative evaluation session took place in Len's classroom, February 23–25. I hadn't realized it before, but he was a master teacher. He came alive in a roomful of kids. Perhaps many of these kids were considered "remedial" and "at-risk" by some, but they clearly loved being in this class.

No doubt about it, the workshop hummed under Len's capable delivery. The students responded well and clearly benefited from the concepts presented in just the ways we had planned. It couldn't have gone better. I wished Suzanne had been there. She'd sent me a note saying she had to beg off to take care of some other things that had come up unexpectedly. Since Dwight and Jane were not free during second period, I had to carry out the evaluation by myself. The results were so good, however, that with just a few minor changes in presentation order and the reformatting of two overheads, we had it!

"Are You Ready?" A Workplace Readiness Workshop - Formative Evaluation Results

Dates: February 23-25, **Time:** 2nd Period **Facilitator:** Len Gold

The purpose of the formative evaluation was to provide an assessment of the effectiveness of workshop activities in producing gains in student learning outcomes. The pilot workshop was presented over a three-day period, 50 minutes per day.

Goal: Students will be able to describe and demonstrate interpersonal communications skills suitable for the workplace.

Learning outcomes:

Students will be able to:

Describe the principles of teamwork
Work as a team to solve a problem
State steps the team used to solve the problem
State different roles people assumed within the group
Recognize personal contributions to group process

Students will be able to:

Determine a process that can be used to resolve conflicts with others
List steps in conflict resolution
Practice listening and speaking skills used in conflict resolution
Practice mediating a conflict

Workshop Activities:

Part 1 Problem-Solving Activities and Teamwork Evaluation

The 28 students in Len's Gold's class were divided into five groups of 5 and 6 students each. All teams satisfactorily resolved the problem-solving tasks, which included completing 3 stations: Crossing the Alligator River, Knots, Survival in the Desert

Part 2 Conflict Resolution

All students participated in role-playing activities both as mediator and as disputants. Seventy-eight percent of the students could list all the steps in conflict resolution process.

Part 3 Guest Speaker

This section of the workshop was not presented during the pilot due to time limitations. These students will attend the formal workshop in March and will hear this presentation at that time.

Part 4 Overall Workshop Assessment

Results from Student Evaluation Form:
A Likert scale was used with ratings from 1 (Strongly Disagree) to 4 (Strongly Agree). The average rating for each question is given below:

	$n = 28$
Overall I thought the workshop provided useful information that will help me in my future work.	3.55
The activities held my interest.	3.63
The workshop was well organized.	3.76
I think that this workshop will be helpful to other students.	3.76

Summary of Responses to Open-Ended Questions:

(Note: Student responses are reproduced in their own language and spelling.)

1. Please comment on the different sections of the Workshop. Which part of the Workshop did you like the best and why?

A majority of students (73.2%) selected the Group problem-solving activities as the one they liked best. Almost all students said that they enjoyed these activities. Comments:

- "Way cool"
- "Let's do this all of the time"
- "This is goofy, but ok"
- "I wish all of my classes could be like yours, Mr. Gold"
- "Dum"

The Conflict Resolution portion of the workshop was seen as valuable by a majority (83%) of the students, with 5.6% listing it as the most important. Comments:

- "I need to medate with Calvin and Veronica so they will leave me alone"
- "Its ok. Maybe we can help stops the fights"
- "Dummer"
- "We need to know how to get along better"

2. Do you have suggestions for improving the workshop?

Comments were largely positive, suggesting that most students felt that the workshop was all right the way it was. Comments:

- " Good work, Gold. No changes."
- "Let's have the workshop during my business accounting class"
- "Have food"

Recommendations

1. Redo the overheads giving the expert's solution to the Survival in the Desert. Use larger type. Use fewer lines per page.

2. Change the order of the activities in the problem-solving section. Put the Survival in the Desert activity between the Alligator River and Knots (the two out-of-seat activities).

I was really beginning to get excited about this. In spite of all my initial doubts, perhaps my first school-based instructional design was going to work! I even looked forward to our workshop presentation next week.

▶ March 1, 3:15 P.M.

Finally, after months of work, our first workshop was grinding to a close. I had been watching the clock for the last half hour and I knew that I was not the only one.

The strawberry blond girl in the seat in front of me was loud in her complaints to her seatmate, "Man, this is so-o-o boring! Why have they got us in this meeting when we're going on to college? What we need is to know how to do well on the SATs and write the best essay on the admission form. Not this junk!"

Her friend returned, "Oh, it wasn't that bad. Got us out of the witch's class anyway. But I guess you're right. I need to get a job this summer. I hear Mrs. Pruitt's students at least do job applications and all that stuff."

Looking around the room, I could see that students were doodling, passing notes, or looking out the windows. Several had their heads on their desks.

Mercifully, the final bell rang signaling the conclusion of the school day. The students didn't wait to be dismissed. They took off in a stampede for the doors. The facilitator, Don McKay, caught my eye and shrugged. Well, I knew he wasn't to blame.

The difference between this and the formative workshop run in Len's class was like night and day. Why had so many things gone wrong?

Invoking ID practice via the Terry Kirkland case

1. List ways to ensure that all stakeholders have been included in the needs assessment.

2. Describe effective strategies for encouraging positive participation from all stakeholders.

3. Describe ways to carry out an in-depth contextual analysis.

4. Describe ways to conduct useful formative evaluations under imperfect field conditions.

5. Suggest strategies that promote effective project management.

Part III

Taking Stock of Your Learning; Setting Your Sights on the Future
by Peggy A. Ertmer

This book would not be complete without asking you, as novice instructional design professionals, to step back from your experiences with the cases in this book and to reflect on the entire case-learning process. Indeed, one of the primary purposes for using case studies as an instructional approach is to facilitate your growing ability to think like designers. This can be accomplished more readily if you take time to reflect, not only on *what* you have learned (the case content) but *how* you learned it (the strategies you used while learning—your case-analysis approach).

▶ Reflection on the case-learning experience

"Experience alone is not the key to learning" (Boud, Keogh, & Walker, 1985, p. 7). The learning that results from the types of situations we presented in this book depends not only on your *experiences* with these problem situations but also on your *reflections* on and evaluation of how you analyzed the design situations. Whereas you may never encounter the same situations as the designers in this book, you will continue to encounter messy problems that require problem-solving skills similar to the ones you used while analyzing these cases. Reflection on the case-learning process will enable you to more readily apply what you have learned from these cases to other contexts and other problems.

Dewey (1933) argued that we learn *more* from reflecting on our experiences than we do from the actual experiences. As mentioned in the introduction to this book, reflection plays an important role during every stage of the learning process—before, during, and after. Reflection *prepares* us for learning, helps us monitor and adjust effort, strategies, and attitude *during* learning, and increases understanding and sense-making *after* learning. According to Wilson and Cole (1991), reflection helps bring meaning to activities that might otherwise be more rote and procedural. Furthermore, reflection can help us learn how to think about our work and the work of others in order to understand it, learn from it, and eventually contribute to new conceptions of it.

To maximize your case-learning experience, I ask you to consider a series of questions regarding *how* you learned from the cases in this book. Think about the following ideas/questions:

▶   What was it like trying to learn from case studies?

>   How interesting, valuable, and relevant was the case approach?

>   How motivating was it?

>   How challenging and/or frustrating was it? What features contributed to the challenge level? Should these features be altered and if so, how?

>   How would you describe your attitude toward using case studies as a learning tool?

▶   Describe your case-analysis approach.

>   What strategies did you use to analyze each case? Did you use a systematic approach, or was it more hit and miss?

>   Did your approach change over the course of the semester and if so, how?

>   What did you do when you hit a "snag"? (Did you give up? Did you consult other resources? Did you talk to other students?)

>   Compare the effort required to analyze and discuss a case with that required to complete other instructional activities, such as writing a paper or completing textbook exercises.

▶   Reflect on how you could improve your approach to case learning.

▶   Now that you have completed a series of cases, what advice would you give to other ID students who were just beginning a course/book like this?

▶ Reflection on the usefulness of the case method as a teaching strategy

Now that you've spent some time grappling with case studies as a learner and have considered the relative benefits and challenges to learning in this way, I'd like to ask you to change hats—to take the perspective of an instructional designer rather than that of a student. (This shouldn't be too difficult—you've been wearing a variety of hats throughout the cases in this book!)

The designers in the cases you've analyzed were confronted with many difficult decisions. Often they had to decide how to present critical information in an interesting and relevant way. Selecting instructional strategies is one of the most crucial steps in the design process. Yet educators continue to complain that "teachers teach the way they were taught," meaning that they tend to use traditional didactic methods to present information, often without even considering whether a lecture would be the most effective means. Instructional strategies often are not selected purposefully. I once had a colleague (an ID student) tell me that whenever she was asked to teach something her first thought, in terms of strategies, was always a lecture. This was how she remembered learning; this was what she was comfortable delivering. She admitted that she had to force herself to consider a wide range of available strategies and to choose one that best fit the goals, learners, and context of the situation.

Hopefully this book has given you a good sample of a very different approach to learning—case-based instruction. You've just spent some time thinking about what that experience was like, in terms of both the benefits and the challenges. Sometimes when I use this approach in my courses, I ask my students to *design* a case as part of their coursework. There are additional benefits for students/designers when they attempt to describe a design situation in such a way that it captures the attention of their peers without leading them to their own preferred solution. This can be a valuable experience, extending the case-learning experience. Furthermore, it gives students the chance to assume the role of both designer and instructor.

Now that you are on the road to becoming instructional designers in your own right, think about how you might be able to use this instructional strategy in the courses you design and the workshops you facilitate. Do you know of any situations that may be particularly appropriate for such an approach? Can you think of situations where this approach would not be appropriate? Are there any specific types of learners that would/would not benefit from this approach? By reflecting on these questions, I hope that when you begin designing/teaching your own courses and workshops, you will feel comfortable using an approach other than the traditional stand-up lecture. Perhaps your first thoughts, when asked to teach, will be "How can I incorporate case studies into this instruction?"

Reflection on the future of case-based instruction in the ID field

Judging by the responses we've had from reviewers, peers, instructors, and students, the use of case-based instruction in the ID field is just beginning. Yet, given that there are no other case books currently available in this field, we were surprised by the number of people who indicated that they already use cases in their courses. It appears as though they have not yet found a professional means for sharing their cases. This *CaseBook* will provide an outlet as well as an impetus to share our design experiences with others.

Text-based cases are still the norm in other professions—business, law, medicine, and more recently, teacher education. They are relatively inexpensive, accessible, and portable. In addition, some disciplines are beginning to experiment with other methods of delivery. Interactive hypermedia video cases have been used in teacher education (e.g., Abell, Cennamo, & Campbell, 1996; Lacey & Merseth, 1993), medical education (Williams, 1993), as well as public health education via interactive museum kiosks (Bell, Bareiss, & Beckwith, 1993–1994).

With the explosion of the use of the World Wide Web (WWW) for instructional purposes and with the introduction of web-based ID cases by Kinzie and her colleagues (Kinzie, Hrabe, & Larsen, 1998), a new and exciting vehicle for ID cases is now available. This method of delivery will make dissemination and use of cases in our field even more likely and must be considered seriously by all who intend to use cases in their future work. Although the Web makes new instructional approaches and new pedagogical features readily available (e.g., video, audio, graphics), it brings with it additional pedagogical issues and concerns. These benefits and concerns are addressed by Kovalchick, Hrabe, Julian, and Kinzie in the remaining sections of this book.

REFERENCES

Abell, S. K., Cennamo, K. S., & Campbell, L. M. (1996). Interactive video cases developed for elementary science methods courses. *Tech Trends, 41*(3), 20–23.

Bell, B., Bareiss, R., & Beckwith, R. (1993–1994). Sickle cell counselor: A prototype goal-based scenario for instruction in a museum environment. *Journal of the Learning Sciences, 3,* 347–386.

Boud, D., Keogh, R., & Walker, D. (Eds.). (1985). *Reflection: Turning experience into learning.* New York: Nichols.

Dewey, J. (1933). *How we think: A restatement of the relation of reflective thinking to the educative process.* Boston: Heath.

Hrabe, M. E., Julian, M. F., Kinzie, M. B., & Kovalchick, A. (1997). *Prescription: Instructional design.* Web-based case available at: http://teach.virginia.edu/go/ITcases

Hrabe, M. E., Larsen, V. A., & Kinzie, M. B. (1996). *The trials of Terry Kirkland.* Web-based case available at: http://teach.virginia.edu/go/ITcases

Kinzie, M. B., Hrabe, M. E., & Larsen, V. A. (1998). An instructional design case event: Exploring issues in professional practice. *Educational Technology Research & Development, 46*(1), 53–71.

Lacey, C. A., & Merseth, K. K. (1993). Cases, hypermedia, and computer networks: Three curricular innovations for teacher education. *Journal of Curriculum Studies, 25,* 543–551.

Williams S. (1993). Putting case-based instruction into context: Examples from legal, business, and medical education *Journal of the Learning Sciences, 2,* 367–427.

Wilson, B., & Cole, P. (1991). A review of cognitive teaching models. *Educational Technology Research and Development, 39*(4), 47–64.

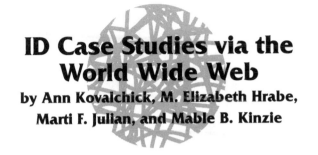

ID Case Studies via the World Wide Web
by Ann Kovalchick, M. Elizabeth Hrabe,
Marti F. Julian, and Mable B. Kinzie

The use of the Web for case-based teaching in ID was first explored at the University of Virginia's Curry School of Education with the introduction of "The Trials of Terry Kirkland" (Hrabe, Larsen, & Kinzie, 1996), designed for the 1996 Instructional Design Case Competition. In 1997 two more Web-based ID cases—"Harvesting Cooperation" (Kovalchick, Julian, Hrabe, & Kinzie, 1997) and "Prescription: Instructional Design" (Hrabe, Julian, Kinzie, & Kovalchick, 1997)—were presented. These cases may be accessed at the following URL:

http://curry.edschool.virginia.edu/go/ITcases

▶ Why design Web-based case studies?

Three significant capabilities are provided to us when we use the World Wide Web for case delivery. These are: (1) the ability to simulate "real-world" complexities, (2) the ability to use multiple media in case presentation, and (3) the ability to use hyperlink/hypertext navigation features.

Realism

Our desire to consider the Web format for case-based instruction grew out of our recognition that to effectively simulate professional practice in the ID profession, the complexities of "real-world" events need to be accurately represented in case materials. Print materials, while familiar and easy to use, essentially lack explicit interactive properties. They allow us to present a description of the ID scenarios but require learners to comprehend events in a more or less sequential manner. Still, it is possible to design print materials to be more discursive, as with the case overviews, case objectives, and key focusing questions used in the cases in this text.

In designing Web-based cases, the aim is to reinforce the generative processes that good narrative facilitates. Presenting material via the Web enhances students' comprehension of text-based descriptions by contextualizing relevant conditions of events and by explicitly prompting linkages among events described within the text. Consequently, real-world events can be presented nonhierarchically. Among the cases mentioned earlier, this was most clearly achieved in "Prescription: Instructional Design," largely due to the use of a floor plan metaphor as an organizing design principle (a concept discussed later).

Given that a primary feature of case-based teaching is its ability to foster connections between an individual's knowledge base and her or his experience, media that facilitate dynamic thinking are especially useful. The efficacy of hypermedia is that "information can be rearranged, analyzed, shifted, and molded to suit the needs of each individual and the context in which material is learned and/or applied" (Borsook & Higgenbotham-Wheat, 1992, p. 10). The range of problems that instructional designers face require that they consider multiple points of view and predict alternative courses of action, often in ill-structured and unpredictable contexts. Web-based instructional materials can recreate these aspects of professional practice.

Multiple Media

A second key aspect of Web-based cases is the ability to present content materials in multiple media formats. In practice, this remains a problematic aspect of using the Web and can be most effectively exploited if case materials are designed for local use at a specified level of technical capacity. As Web technology develops, the ability to present audio, video, and animated media will be simplified. Nevertheless, it is worth exploring options for using multiple media sources within Web-based cases. Often it is the ancillary materials such as interview clips, simulated documents, and relevant graphics that lend authenticity to case scenarios. Providing an environment rich in artifacts that support the case issues and objectives allows students to simulate the processes of considering hypotheses and applying theories based on empirical evidence as in an actual design scenario. In addition, ancillary materials provide a point of contact for collaborative processes, prompting students to weigh the importance of secondary information and to articulate their individual arguments for or against its inclusion in defining the design solution.

Hyperlink Navigation

Finally, the Web's ability to prompt linkages among ideas, events, and artifacts via hypertext and hyperlinks can direct learners to construct and to perceive patterns of meaning among disparate sources of information. Instructional designers are often called on to create order and coherence out of nonfunctioning conditions. This requires the use of analytical processes to both generalize and discriminate. Hyper-navigation through a web of data relating to an ID problem can foster both inductive and deductive strategies of discovery, thereby expanding the instructional designer's toolkit of methods. For example, proven principles of ID methods can be systematically analyzed as they are woven into (or found lacking in!) the case narrative. In this way, ID students can deductively test a variety of ID models and processes through the logical application of their constituent parts. Although designers often face a range of instructional conditions, it is important for novice designers to recognize the utility of formal models as a starting point for mapping out what is known and unknown about a given design scenario.

While the skills and knowledge of formal reasoning used to problem-solve a design situation are an essential aspect of professional practice, designers must also develop the insight and sensitivity to recognize particular conditions. Faced with a complex design problem, ID students can define given aspects of the problem and consider how local knowledge (the resources, talents, and skills represented by the fictionalized case characters) can contribute to developing a design solution. The rich context provided in Web-based cases can be especially useful for prompting novice designers to look beyond the obvious in cases where the application of common ID assumptions appear to have failed. In this way, ID students can learn to generate "grounded theory" to guide their decision-making process in unique situations. For example, in "The Trials of Terry Kirkland," the designer Terry Kirkland has not conducted an adequate analysis of the sociocultural context in which the ID is developed and implemented. Had Kirkland understood the particular history of the group of individuals who had been developing the training, she might have recognized that key individuals were reacting to events that preceded her involvement. While students who have used the case have provided thoughts on how her design might have benefited from a contextual analysis, they were also prompted to cite specific ways she could have made use of this local knowledge had a more thorough contextual analysis been done. Consequently, it would not be enough for ID students to recognize that a contextual analysis is necessary, but they should also be able to determine how the findings can influence the parameters of the given situation.

Used properly, hyperlinks also offer the possibility of providing various levels of scaffolding according to student needs. Although an advantage of Web-based cases is the abundance of information surrounding an ID scenario that can be provided, this may be an overwhelming amount of information to novice designers. Depending on the instructor's goals, navigation through the information can be teacher-led and highly directed, or may be student-centered in that students are permitted to explore independently or in small groups. Hyperlinks can also allow the instructor to regulate the presentation of material by presenting the design scenario in small, incremental steps. The instructor may anticipate student difficulties with certain aspects of case specifics—or of an ID model used to analyze the case—and increase the level of task difficulty as necessary. Instructors and students can model the use of the case and think aloud about choices—points and decisions relevant to ID problem solving. Depending on how hyperlinks are navigated, instructors may use various prompts from checklists to open-ended reflections to determine student mastery of both concrete and theoretical aspects of ID.

▶ Activities for comparing text cases and multimedia web-based cases

To develop an appreciation for the possibilities inherent in using Web-based case studies for discussion by students in the classroom, we have provided the following activity based on the knowledge-as-design analysis theory of Perkins (1987). Perkins suggests four primary questions useful for analyzing a design configuration. These are:

1.   What is its purpose?
2.   What is its structure?
3.   What are model cases of it?
4.   What are arguments that explain and evaluate it?

We have addressed question 3 by providing two model cases in a print format in this text. These are "Julie Tatano: Harvesting Cooperation" and "Terry Kirkland." You may find a Web-based version of "Harvesting Cooperation" (Kovalchick et al., 1997) and "The Trials of Terry Kirkland" (Hrabe et al., 1996) together with a third, "Prescription: Instructional Design" (Hrabe et al., 1997), at the following URL:

http://teach.virginia.edu/go/ITcases

Now, we'd like you to consider the other three questions through the following activity.

Materials Note: This exercise uses the Case Study Analysis charts found in the appendix. You will need to fill these charts out for each type of case-study design. Therefore, we suggest that you photocopy the charts before you begin the exercise.

▶ Comparison of web- and print-based cases

Part I.

1.   Read the text version of "Julie Tatano" or "Terry Kirkland."
2.   Fill out a copy of the "Case Study Analysis Part I: Characteristics" chart for the *text* version of the case you have chosen. It is very important to appreciate the design qualities of each case as a unique entity. You may want to brainstorm your ideas with colleagues.
3.   What are the important design features (not content) of the text version? List as many as you can. Then for each feature you have listed,

determine how the feature facilitates the comprehension of the content. For example, one feature of a text case might have to do with the page layout. What size are the paragraphs? How are they arranged? If they are long, does that make them easy or difficult to read?

4. Now describe the strengths and weaknesses of the design. For example, a strength might be that text cases are easily portable.

5. Finally, think about this design as a whole. What are the best ways to use text cases?

Remember that any kind of analysis is an iterative process. For example, you may need to revisit the "purpose" section of the chart after you have done some further study of the features and design principles that inform the case study.

Don't go on to Part II just yet.

6. Now examine the Web-based version of the same case.

Fill out a second "Case Study Analysis Part I: Characteristics" chart for the *Web* version of the case you have chosen. Proceed through the analysis as you did earlier. Possible areas for inclusion in your design analysis of the Web-based case might include some of the following: ease of use, need for instructions, portability, accessibility, role of hyperlinks, use of metaphor as organizing idea, layers of complexity present, characterization, and role of photographs, audio, and video.

Part II.

7. When you have completed Part I for both types of case design, lay your analysis sheets side by side and compare each section. What do you notice about the similarities? What differences do you notice? Is there any important design issue that you have not addressed?

8. Turn to the "Case Study Analysis Part II: Comparison" chart to note the similarities and differences. Write down any conclusions you have come to.

9. Now, take a few minutes to reflect on the two analyses you have just carried out. What have you learned about case design? Apply what you have discovered by writing a brief reaction paper, addressing the pros and cons of using the Web for designing instruction.

▶ Discussion

We strongly believe that text cases and Web-based cases are not in competition. As you have seen, each design has a different set of purposes and functions that facilitate understanding. Consider an important observation based on our own experience in designing multimedia case studies for use by students in the classroom and by participants in a case competition: sooner or later in the case-analysis process Web-based cases *become* text-based cases. As you have probably observed, it is difficult to read text documents presented on a computer monitor. Thus, all of our users have indicated that they download and print out the cases for closer reading (Kinzie, et al., 1997).

Why then have multimedia Web-based cases if students end by reading text versions of them? In the following section, we describe some of the unique contributions the use of Web-based cases have made to facilitating learning in the ID classroom.

▶ Using Web-based cases in the classroom and in competition environments

How can ID students make greatest use of multimedia Web-based cases? We have explored the use of such cases with students in two widely dissimilar environments: in the classroom and in two national ID case competitions. See Kinzie et al. (1997) for a discussion of our first national case competition. Our experience with students in both venues suggests that there are several instructional benefits to innovative uses of Web-based case studies.

Active immersion in the world of a case study

Multimedia cases may best be suited to presenting multilayered, complex, ill-defined situations in which a variety of issues may face an instructional designer against a background of subtly revealed political, cultural, and personal influences. Students may then take several class periods to "live" with the issues presented in such cases. Teachers can flexibly accommodate the particular needs of the class by choosing which issues to pursue in depth. Through the use of class activities and leading questions during class discussion, the instructor can guide students through a complicated case, suggesting possible directions for exploration, adjusting perceptions, and raising contrary ideas when needed. More advanced students may be able to take these leaps independently.

Collaboration

Our experience with these large, diffuse case studies suggests that they are most useful when analyzed by students working in teams. Teams of four or five members appear to be most effective. Smaller groups may lack the wealth of internal resources derived from pooling the experience and expertise of individual group members, while larger teams tend to become unwieldy. Students have expressed enthusiasm for the dynamic process that often develops during such collaboration. The presentation of multiple perspectives during team deliberations and the act of coming to consensus are perceived by students as useful in their development as professionals (Kinzie et al., 1997).

The success of team collaboration within classes has led to frequent requests for collaboration across sites. Students enjoy sharing case responses with teams from other institutions. We have attempted to further such communication asynchronously through e-mail and posting comments/responses to the Web site. Other possibilities for cross-site collaboration might include the use of newsgroups or such synchronous communication as could be provided by video conferencing or chat rooms.

Role-playing

The availability of this technology, which can facilitate communication over distance, together with the interactive nature of the multimedia Web cases has led to the desire by students to overcome the "static" nature of the case-study model by interacting directly with characters from the case. Just as instructional designers in practice have the ability to ask questions of stakeholders and others, so students involved in a case analysis wish to have the ability to speak with important characters in the case. Certainly the possibilities exist for such role-playing. The available technology could permit experts from the field or even instructors to answer student questions by taking on the perspective of a case character either in "online real time" or in a mailing list format. We have recently been tentatively exploring such "interactivity" with "Harvesting Cooperation."

Multiple perspectives

In addition to the case analyses shared among teams within a class and across sites, the Web allows us to present expert opinions from ID professionals or from fields represented in a particular case. These can be made available at the case Web site. Thus, in "Terry Kirkland" it is possible to hear from a public school administrator and an instructional designer who works in a school setting, while in "Harvesting Cooperation" we can hear from an extension agent as well as a designer connected to a large university. These expert perspectives serve to provide other perspectives on the case and widen students' understanding about resources and contacts for developing professional knowledge in real-world situations.

Web-based research

Finally, instructional designers need to be aware of a multitude of resources and materials they will need for research and design development when they are hired to create content for areas in which they lack expertise. In a Web-based case study, it is possible to embed links leading to Internet resources that can aid students in creating their own design solutions to a case. Rich content materials are available on the Web, as are sources for expert contacts. Pointing students toward the Web as a significant resource can enhance their learning experiences. In "Julie Tatano: Harvesting Cooperation" we endeavored to do this by including in the story a list of URLs that provided content information about the theme of Integrated Pest Management.

The availability of new media delivery systems offers additional possibilities for using case-based teaching in ID. Hypermedia technologies such as the Web can enhance case-based teaching by providing a means for introducing authentic contextual cues, prompting students to actively employ analytical and organizing skills as they navigate through the Web-based case, and by presenting information in multiple media formats. Web-based cases thus offer an additional means of closing the gap between theory and practice.

REFERENCES

Borsook, T. K., & Higgenbotham-Wheat, N. (1992). *The psychology of hypermedia: A conceptual framework for R & D.* Paper presented at the 1992 National Convention of the Association for Educational Communications and Technology (AECT), Washington, DC.

Hrabe, M.E., Julian, M.F., Kinzie, M.B., & Kovalchick, A. (1997). *Prescription: Instructional design.* Web-based case available at: http://teach. virginia.edu/go/ITcases

Hrabe, M.E., Larsen, V.A., & Kinzie, M.B. (1996). *The trials of Terry Kirkland.* Web-based case available at: http://teach. virginia.edu/go/ITcases

Kinzie, M. B. Hrabe, M. E. & Larsen, V. A. (February 1997). *An instructional design case event: Exploring issues in professional practice.* Paper presented at the annual meeting of the Association for Educational Communications & Technology (AECT), Albuquerque, NM, 1997.

Kovalchick, A., Julian, M. F., Hrabe, M. E., & Kinzie, M. B. (1997). *Harvesting cooperation.* Web-based case available at: http://teach.virginia.edu/go/ITcases

Perkins, D. N. (1987). Knowledge as design: Teaching thinking through content. In J. B. Baron & R. J. Sternberg (Eds.), *Teaching thinking skills: Theory and practice* (pp. 64–77). New York: Freeman, 1987.

Appendix

Case Study Analysis Part I: Characteristics
(adapted by authors from D.N. Perkins)

1. Case Study Design: Text-based design   Web-based design

2. Title: _____

3. Purposes: (what you conceive to be the instructional purposes of the case, taking into consideration the overall design and format in which it is presented)

1. _____
2. _____
3. _____
4. _____

4. Structure (list of features)   How each feature facilitates content comprehension.

1. _____   1. _____
2. _____   2. _____
3. _____   3. _____
4. _____   4. _____
5. _____   5. _____
6. _____   6. _____
7. _____   7. _____
8. _____   8. _____
9. _____   9. _____
10. _____   10. _____
11. _____   11. _____
12. _____   12. _____
13. _____   13. _____
14. _____   14. _____
15. _____   15. _____

5. Evaluate: What are **strengths** of the design structure

1. _____
2. _____
3. _____
4. _____
5. _____
6. _____
7. _____
8. _____
9. _____
10. _____

6. Evaluate: What are **weaknesses** that may result from the design structure

1. _____
2. _____
3. _____
4. _____
5. _____
6. _____
7. _____
8. _____
9. _____
10. _____

7. Principles for effective use: What are the best ways to use this design/structure?

_____
_____
_____
_____
_____

8. Alternative examples of these principles?

_____
_____
_____
_____
_____

Case Study Analysis Part II: Comparison

Title: _____

1. Similarities: Generally, how are the designs similar?

_____
_____
_____
_____
_____
_____

2. Differences: Generally, how do the designs differ?

_____
_____
_____
_____
_____
_____

3. Concluding statement on the use of text and Web-based cases

_____
_____
_____
_____
_____
_____